D1987067

Power purchase agreement
Complete Self-Assessment Guide

The guidance in this Self-Assessment is based on Power purchase agreement best practices and standards in business process architecture, design and quality management. The guidance is also based on the professional judgment of the individual collaborators listed in the Acknowledgments.

http://theartofservice.com
service@theartofservice.com

Table of Contents

About The Art of Service

The Art of Service, Business Process Architects since 2000, is dedicated to helping stakeholders achieve excellence.

Defining, designing, creating, and implementing a process to solve a stakeholders challenge or meet an objective is the most valuable role… In EVERY group, company, organization and department.

Unless you're talking a one-time, single-use project, there should be a process. Whether that process is managed and implemented by humans, AI, or a combination of the two, it needs to be designed by someone with a complex enough perspective to ask the right questions.

Someone capable of asking the right questions and step back and say, 'What are we really trying to accomplish here? And is there a different way to look at it?'

With The Art of Service's Standard Requirements Self-Assessments, we empower people who can do just that — whether their title is marketer, entrepreneur, manager, salesperson, consultant, Business Process Manager, executive assistant, IT Manager, CIO etc... —they are the people who rule the future. They are people who watch the process as it happens, and ask the right questions to make the process work better.

Contact us when you need any support with this Self-Assessment and any help with templates, blue-prints and examples of standard documents you might need:

http://theartofservice.com
service@theartofservice.com

Acknowledgments

This checklist was developed under the auspices of The Art of Service, chaired by Gerardus Blokdyk.

Representatives from several client companies participated in the preparation of this Self-Assessment.

In addition, we are thankful for the design and printing services provided.

Included Resources - how to access

Included with your purchase of the book is the Power purchase agreement Self-Assessment Spreadsheet Dashboard which contains all questions and Self-Assessment areas and auto-generates insights, graphs, and project RACI planning - all with examples to get you started right away.

How? Simply send an email to
access@theartofservice.com
with this books' title in the subject to get the Power purchase agreement Self Assessment Tool right away.

You will receive the following contents with New and Updated specific criteria:

- The latest quick edition of the book in PDF
- The latest complete edition of the book in PDF, which criteria correspond to the criteria in...
- The Self-Assessment Excel Dashboard, and...
- Example pre-filled Self-Assessment Excel Dashboard to get familiar with results generation
- In-depth specific Checklists covering the topic
- Project management checklists and templates to assist with implementation

INCLUDES LIFETIME SELF ASSESSMENT UPDATES

Every self assessment comes with Lifetime Updates and Lifetime Free Updated Books. Lifetime Updates is an industry-first feature which allows you to receive verified self assessment updates, ensuring you always have the most accurate information at your fingertips.

Get it now- you will be glad you did - do it now, before you forget.

Send an email to **access@theartofservice.com** with this books' title in the subject to get the Power purchase agreement Self Assessment Tool right away.

Your feedback is invaluable to us

If you recently bought this book, we would love to hear from you! You can do this by writing a review on amazon (or the online store where you purchased this book) about your last purchase! As part of our continual service improvement process, we love to hear real client experiences and feedback.

How does it work?
To post a review on Amazon, just log in to your account and click on the Create Your Own Review button (under Customer Reviews) of the relevant product page. You can find examples of product reviews in Amazon. If you purchased from another online store, simply follow their procedures.

What happens when I submit my review?
Once you have submitted your review, send us an email at review@theartofservice.com with the link to your review so we can properly thank you for your feedback.

Purpose of this Self-Assessment

This Self-Assessment has been developed to improve understanding of the requirements and elements of Power purchase agreement, based on best practices and standards in business process architecture, design and quality management.

It is designed to allow for a rapid Self-Assessment to determine how closely existing management practices and procedures correspond to the elements of the Self-Assessment.

The criteria of requirements and elements of Power purchase agreement have been rephrased in the format of a Self-Assessment questionnaire, with a seven-criterion scoring system, as explained in this document.

In this format, even with limited background knowledge of Power purchase agreement, a manager can quickly review existing operations to determine how they measure up to the standards. This in turn can serve as the starting point of a 'gap analysis' to identify management tools or system elements that might usefully be implemented in the organization to help improve overall performance.

How to use the Self-Assessment

On the following pages are a series of questions to identify to what extent your Power purchase agreement initiative is complete in comparison to the requirements set in standards.

To facilitate answering the questions, there is a space in front of each question to enter a score on a scale of '1' to '5'.

1 Strongly Disagree

2 Disagree

3 Neutral

4 Agree

5 Strongly Agree

Read the question and rate it with the following in front of mind:

**'In my belief,
the answer to this question is clearly defined'.**

There are two ways in which you can choose to interpret this statement;

1. how aware are you that the answer to the question is clearly defined
2. for more in-depth analysis you can choose to gather

evidence and confirm the answer to the question. This obviously will take more time, most Self-Assessment users opt for the first way to interpret the question and dig deeper later on based on the outcome of the overall Self-Assessment.

A score of '1' would mean that the answer is not clear at all, where a '5' would mean the answer is crystal clear and defined. Leave emtpy when the question is not applicable or you don't want to answer it, you can skip it without affecting your score. Write your score in the space provided.

After you have responded to all the appropriate statements in each section, compute your average score for that section, using the formula provided, and round to the nearest tenth. Then transfer to the corresponding spoke in the Power purchase agreement Scorecard on the second next page of the Self-Assessment.

Your completed Power purchase agreement Scorecard will give you a clear presentation of which Power purchase agreement areas need attention.

Power purchase agreement Scorecard Example

Example of how the finalized Scorecard can look like:

Power purchase agreement Scorecard

Your Scores:

BEGINNING OF THE SELF-ASSESSMENT:

CRITERION #1: RECOGNIZE

INTENT: Be aware of the need for change. Recognize that there is an unfavorable variation, problem or symptom.

In my belief, the answer to this question is clearly defined:

5 Strongly Agree

4 Agree

3 Neutral

2 Disagree

1 Strongly Disagree

1. What vendors make products that address the Power purchase agreement needs?
<--- Score

2. How do you take a forward-looking perspective in identifying Power purchase agreement research related to market response and models?
<--- Score

3. Are you dealing with any of the same issues today as yesterday? What can you do about this?
<--- Score

4. Do you know what you need to know about Power purchase agreement?
<--- Score

5. To what extent does each concerned units management team recognize Power purchase agreement as an effective investment?
<--- Score

6. When a Power purchase agreement manager recognizes a problem, what options are available?
<--- Score

7. What is the smallest subset of the problem you can usefully solve?
<--- Score

8. Does your organization need more Power purchase agreement education?
<--- Score

9. Which Accessible Media Producer (AMP) can be used to obtain the needed format(s)?
<--- Score

10. Are overbillings recognized by contractor?
<--- Score

11. How many performance measures need to be adopted?
<--- Score

12. What situation(s) led to this Power purchase agreement Self Assessment?
<--- Score

13. What is the problem or issue?
<--- Score

14. Who defines the rules in relation to any given issue?
<--- Score

15. What resources are needed to achieve the stated objectives?
<--- Score

16. What barriers have been identified to making effective use of performance measurement and are those barriers being addressed?
<--- Score

17. Are controls defined to recognize and contain problems?
<--- Score

18. Do you need to acquire outside assistance and do you have budget for this?
<--- Score

19. How much are sponsors, customers, partners, stakeholders involved in Power purchase agreement? In other words, what are the risks, if Power purchase agreement does not deliver successfully?
<--- Score

20. Have you identified your Power purchase agreement key performance indicators?

<--- Score

21. Do we have the needed human talent to meet the requirements?
<--- Score

22. Are there Power purchase agreement problems defined?
<--- Score

23. Do any of your existing strategies or initiatives need to be amended or deleted?
<--- Score

24. What problems are you facing and how do you consider Power purchase agreement will circumvent those obstacles?
<--- Score

25. To what extent would your organization benefit from being recognized as a award recipient?
<--- Score

26. What information do users need?
<--- Score

27. Does the system identify the receipt and expenditure of funds separately for each grant or contract?
<--- Score

28. Will currently occupied space (especially leased space) still be needed, in whole or in part, upon lease expiration?
<--- Score

29. What tools and technologies are needed for a custom Power purchase agreement project?
<--- Score

30. We have identified existing contractual relationships (UCs) with external vendors.
<--- Score

31. What do you need to start doing?
<--- Score

32. Do you have/need 24-hour access to key personnel?
<--- Score

33. How does it fit into your organizational needs and tasks?
<--- Score

34. How are you going to measure success?
<--- Score

35. Are your goals realistic? Do you need to redefine your problem? Perhaps the problem has changed or maybe you have reached your goal and need to set a new one?
<--- Score

36. How can auditing be a preventative security measure?
<--- Score

37. What actual uses and effects of performance measurement were identified?
<--- Score

38. What prevents you from making the changes you know will make you a more effective Power purchase agreement leader?
<--- Score

39. When is a budget needed?
<--- Score

40. How do you assess your Power purchase agreement workforce capability and capacity needs, including skills, competencies, and staffing levels?
<--- Score

41. Will a response program recognize when a crisis occurs and provide some level of response?
<--- Score

42. What are your needs in relation to Power purchase agreement skills, labor, equipment, and markets?
<--- Score

43. Will new equipment/products be required to facilitate Power purchase agreement delivery, for example is new software needed?
<--- Score

44. What are the expected benefits of Power purchase agreement to the business?
<--- Score

45. How is the quality of performance information perceived, and how have performance measurement quality issues been addressed?
<--- Score

46. What training and capacity building actions are

needed to implement proposed reforms?
<--- Score

47. What are the timeframes required to resolve each of the issues/problems?
<--- Score

48. Does the company offer flexible collection options to meet your business needs and budget?
<--- Score

49. Do you need to avoid or amend any Power purchase agreement activities?
<--- Score

50. Is it clear when you think of the day ahead of you what activities and tasks you need to complete?
<--- Score

51. Who else hopes to benefit from it?
<--- Score

52. If a separate bank account is not maintained, can the grant/contract funds and related expenses be readily identified?
<--- Score

53. What would happen if Power purchase agreement weren't done?
<--- Score

54. What extra resources will you need?
<--- Score

55. What else needs to be measured?
<--- Score

56. For your Power purchase agreement project, identify and describe the business environment, is there more than one layer to the business environment?
<--- Score

57. What activities does the governance board need to consider?
<--- Score

58. Identification of the reach, frequency, and message weights sought. what will be the geographical allocation of the media budget and why?
<--- Score

59. Will Power purchase agreement deliverables need to be tested and, if so, by whom?
<--- Score

60. Are there any revenue recognition issues?
<--- Score

61. Who had the original idea?
<--- Score

62. Looking at each person individually – does every one have the qualities which are needed to work in this group?
<--- Score

63. Will it solve real problems?
<--- Score

64. Are there recognized Power purchase agreement

problems?
<--- Score

65. Can management personnel recognize the monetary benefit of Power purchase agreement?
<--- Score

66. As a sponsor, customer or management, how important is it to meet goals, objectives?
<--- Score

67. What are the minority interests and what amount of minority interests can be recognized?
<--- Score

68. Think about the people you identified for your Power purchase agreement project and the project responsibilities you would assign to them. what kind of training do you think they would need to perform these responsibilities effectively?
<--- Score

69. Do we need CAPM for capital budgeting?
<--- Score

70. Should you invest in industry-recognized qualications?
<--- Score

71. What are the business objectives to be achieved with Power purchase agreement?
<--- Score

72. Can the facility manager alter the contract and payment terms in the event of revenue shortfall or changes in operational hours?

<--- Score

73. Are there any specific expectations or concerns about the Power purchase agreement team, Power purchase agreement itself?
<--- Score

74. What does Power purchase agreement success mean to the stakeholders?
<--- Score

75. Does our organization need the program, and if so, are there alternative means of accomplishing the desired objectives?
<--- Score

76. Who needs to know about Power purchase agreement?
<--- Score

77. Consider your own Power purchase agreement project, what types of organizational problems do you think might be causing or affecting your problem, based on the work done so far?
<--- Score

78. What should be considered when identifying available resources, constraints, and deadlines?
<--- Score

79. How are the Power purchase agreement's objectives aligned to the organization's overall business strategy?
<--- Score

80. Are employees recognized or rewarded for

performance that demonstrates the highest levels of integrity?
<--- Score

81. Is the need for organizational change recognized?
<--- Score

82. Who are your key stakeholders who need to sign off?
<--- Score

83. Do you need different information or graphics?
<--- Score

84. Are problem definition and motivation clearly presented?
<--- Score

85. Who needs what information?
<--- Score

86. What needs to be done?
<--- Score

87. If you're targeting an internal audience - which individuals, teams or departments do you need to reach within the organization?
<--- Score

88. How do you identify the kinds of information that you will need?
<--- Score

89. Does Power purchase agreement create potential expectations in other areas that need to be recognized and considered?

<--- Score

Add up total points for this section:
_____ = Total points for this section

Divided by: ______ (number of statements answered) = ______ Average score for this section

Transfer your score to the Power purchase agreement Index at the beginning of the Self-Assessment.

CRITERION #2: DEFINE:

INTENT: Formulate the business problem. Define the problem, needs and objectives.

In my belief, the answer to this question is clearly defined:

5 Strongly Agree

4 Agree

3 Neutral

2 Disagree

1 Strongly Disagree

1. Are task requirements clearly defined?
<--- Score

2. Has anyone else (internal or external to the organization) attempted to solve this problem or a similar one before? If so, what knowledge can be leveraged from these previous efforts?
<--- Score

3. Is the improvement team aware of the different versions of a process: what they think it is vs. what it actually is vs. what it should be vs. what it could be?
<--- Score

4. Scope of sensitive information?
<--- Score

5. What system do you use for gathering Power purchase agreement information?
<--- Score

6. In what way can you redefine the criteria of choice clients have in your category in your favor?
<--- Score

7. Who defines (or who defined) the rules and roles?
<--- Score

8. Have all basic functions of Power purchase agreement been defined?
<--- Score

9. What are the Roles and Responsibilities for each team member and its leadership? Where is this documented?
<--- Score

10. Is Power purchase agreement required?
<--- Score

11. Is there a critical path to deliver Power purchase agreement results?
<--- Score

12. What is the context?

<--- Score

13. What are the rough order estimates on cost savings/opportunities that Power purchase agreement brings?
<--- Score

14. Who are the Power purchase agreement improvement team members, including Management Leads and Coaches?
<--- Score

15. How would you define the culture at your organization, how susceptible is it to Power purchase agreement changes?
<--- Score

16. Is there a completed, verified, and validated high-level 'as is' (not 'should be' or 'could be') business process map?
<--- Score

17. Has the Power purchase agreement work been fairly and/or equitably divided and delegated among team members who are qualified and capable to perform the work? Has everyone contributed?
<--- Score

18. How will the Power purchase agreement team and the organization measure complete success of Power purchase agreement?
<--- Score

19. Have the customer needs been translated into specific, measurable requirements? How?
<--- Score

20. How often are the team meetings?
<--- Score

21. Are there different segments of customers?
<--- Score

22. What customer feedback methods were used to solicit their input?
<--- Score

23. Has everyone on the team, including the team leaders, been properly trained?
<--- Score

24. Are roles and responsibilities formally defined?
<--- Score

25. Are business processes mapped?
<--- Score

26. If substitutes have been appointed, have they been briefed on the Power purchase agreement goals and received regular communications as to the progress to date?
<--- Score

27. What key business process output measure(s) does Power purchase agreement leverage and how?
<--- Score

28. Will team members regularly document their Power purchase agreement work?
<--- Score

29. What is the definition of success?

<--- Score

30. Is the program compatible with the mission, role, and scope of the organization?
<--- Score

31. Are customer(s) identified and segmented according to their different needs and requirements?
<--- Score

32. Have all of the relationships been defined properly?
<--- Score

33. Is the current 'as is' process being followed? If not, what are the discrepancies?
<--- Score

34. What was the context?
<--- Score

35. Are there any constraints known that bear on the ability to perform Power purchase agreement work? How is the team addressing them?
<--- Score

36. Is the scope of Power purchase agreement defined?
<--- Score

37. How did the Power purchase agreement manager receive input to the development of a Power purchase agreement improvement plan and the estimated completion dates/times of each activity?
<--- Score

38. How is the team tracking and documenting its work?
<--- Score

39. How do you gather Power purchase agreement requirements?
<--- Score

40. Is consolidation of unrelated, but geographically proximate program requirements an option?
<--- Score

41. Are approval levels defined for contracts and supplements to contracts?
<--- Score

42. Are team charters developed?
<--- Score

43. Has your scope been defined?
<--- Score

44. What specifically is the problem? Where does it occur? When does it occur? What is its extent?
<--- Score

45. What is out-of-scope initially?
<--- Score

46. Do the problem and goal statements meet the SMART criteria (specific, measurable, attainable, relevant, and time-bound)?
<--- Score

47. Does the scope remain the same?

<--- Score

48. What critical content must be communicated – who, what, when, where, and how?
<--- Score

49. How will variation in the actual durations of each activity be dealt with to ensure that the expected Power purchase agreement results are met?
<--- Score

50. What are the dynamics of the communication plan?
<--- Score

51. Will this project require Capital Budget funding?
<--- Score

52. We know our volumes and types of consumed services, and the correlating budget requirement
<--- Score

53. What are the compelling business reasons for embarking on Power purchase agreement?
<--- Score

54. What is the scope of Power purchase agreement?
<--- Score

55. What happens if Power purchase agreement's scope changes?
<--- Score

56. What is the scope of the Power purchase agreement effort?

<--- Score

57. What scope to assess?
<--- Score

58. How do you think the partners involved in Power purchase agreement would have defined success?
<--- Score

59. How and when will the baselines be defined?
<--- Score

60. Are audit criteria, scope, frequency and methods defined?
<--- Score

61. Is full participation by members in regularly held team meetings guaranteed?
<--- Score

62. What capital will be required?
<--- Score

63. Are resources adequate for the scope?
<--- Score

64. Has a high-level 'as is' process map been completed, verified and validated?
<--- Score

65. Does existing space (capacity) exist which could be used to meet new or emerging requirements?
<--- Score

66. What sources do you use to gather information for

a Power purchase agreement study?
<--- Score

67. Is data collected and displayed to better understand customer(s) critical needs and requirements.
<--- Score

68. Do we have the required technology?
<--- Score

69. How do you manage scope?
<--- Score

70. Will team members perform Power purchase agreement work when assigned and in a timely fashion?
<--- Score

71. How was the 'as is' process map developed, reviewed, verified and validated?
<--- Score

72. Are required metrics defined, what are they?
<--- Score

73. How do you hand over Power purchase agreement context?
<--- Score

74. Is Power purchase agreement currently on schedule according to the plan?
<--- Score

75. Are improvement team members fully trained on Power purchase agreement?

<--- Score

76. Why are you doing Power purchase agreement and what is the scope?
<--- Score

77. Has the improvement team collected the 'voice of the customer' (obtained feedback – qualitative and quantitative)?
<--- Score

78. What is out of scope?
<--- Score

79. What are the tasks and definitions?
<--- Score

80. Is there regularly 100% attendance at the team meetings? If not, have appointed substitutes attended to preserve cross-functionality and full representation?
<--- Score

81. Is a fully trained team formed, supported, and committed to work on the Power purchase agreement improvements?
<--- Score

82. What scope do you want your strategy to cover?
<--- Score

83. What Power purchase agreement requirements should be gathered?
<--- Score

84. Is the team formed and are team leaders (Coaches

and Management Leads) assigned?
<--- Score

85. Is it clearly defined in and to your organization what you do?
<--- Score

86. Who is gathering Power purchase agreement information?
<--- Score

87. Requires targets or goals. Who sets them – Producers or Government?
<--- Score

88. When are meeting minutes sent out? Who is on the distribution list?
<--- Score

89. Is there a completed SIPOC representation, describing the Suppliers, Inputs, Process, Outputs, and Customers?
<--- Score

90. Has/have the customer(s) been identified?
<--- Score

91. What constraints exist that might impact the team?
<--- Score

92. Do you all define Power purchase agreement in the same way?
<--- Score

93. Is there a Power purchase agreement

management charter, including business case, problem and goal statements, scope, milestones, roles and responsibilities, communication plan?
<--- Score

94. Do we have the required technology?
<--- Score

95. What are the record-keeping requirements of Power purchase agreement activities?
<--- Score

96. Has a project plan, Gantt chart, or similar been developed/completed?
<--- Score

97. How does the Power purchase agreement manager ensure against scope creep?
<--- Score

98. What defines best in class?
<--- Score

99. What is in scope?
<--- Score

100. Is scope creep really all bad news?
<--- Score

101. Are accountability and ownership for Power purchase agreement clearly defined?
<--- Score

102. How can the value of Power purchase agreement be defined?
<--- Score

103. Are customers identified and high impact areas defined?
<--- Score

104. Are different versions of process maps needed to account for the different types of inputs?
<--- Score

105. Is the team adequately staffed with the desired cross-functionality? If not, what additional resources are available to the team?
<--- Score

106. What baselines are required to be defined and managed?
<--- Score

107. What would be the goal or target for a Power purchase agreement's improvement team?
<--- Score

108. Requires reporting from Producers. Defines reporting requirements?
<--- Score

109. How do you keep key subject matter experts in the loop?
<--- Score

110. Is Power purchase agreement linked to key business goals and objectives?
<--- Score

111. When was the Power purchase agreement start date?

<--- Score

112. Does the team have regular meetings?
<--- Score

113. Have specific policy objectives been defined?
<--- Score

114. When is the estimated completion date?
<--- Score

115. Has the direction changed at all during the course of Power purchase agreement? If so, when did it change and why?
<--- Score

116. Is the Power purchase agreement scope manageable?
<--- Score

117. Is the team equipped with available and reliable resources?
<--- Score

118. Is the team sponsored by a champion or business leader?
<--- Score

119. Has a team charter been developed and communicated?
<--- Score

120. What is in the scope and what is not in scope?
<--- Score

121. What are the boundaries of the scope? What is in

bounds and what is not? What is the start point? What is the stop point?
<--- Score

122. Is the Power purchase agreement scope complete and appropriately sized?
<--- Score

Add up total points for this section:
_____ = Total points for this section

Divided by: ______ (number of statements answered) = ______ Average score for this section

Transfer your score to the Power purchase agreement Index at the beginning of the Self-Assessment.

CRITERION #3: MEASURE:

INTENT: Gather the correct data.
Measure the current performance and
evolution of the situation.

In my belief, the answer to this
question is clearly defined:

5 Strongly Agree

4 Agree

3 Neutral

2 Disagree

1 Strongly Disagree

1. What measurements are being captured?
<--- Score

2. How do you measure success?
<--- Score

3. What are the types and number of measures to use?
<--- Score

4. What are your customers expectations and measures?
<--- Score

5. Are there any easy-to-implement alternatives to Power purchase agreement? Sometimes other solutions are available that do not require the cost implications of a full-blown project?
<--- Score

6. How do your measurements capture actionable Power purchase agreement information for use in exceeding your customers expectations and securing your customers engagement?
<--- Score

7. What could cause you to change course?
<--- Score

8. Why do the measurements/indicators matter?
<--- Score

9. Number of firms with identical costs and a given demand curve?
<--- Score

10. What are your key Power purchase agreement indicators that you will measure, analyze and track?
<--- Score

11. Contract Analysis: Am I complying with my existing negotiated contract terms?
<--- Score

12. Are missed Power purchase agreement opportunities costing your organization money?

<--- Score

13. How do you aggregate measures across priorities?
<--- Score

14. What do you measure and why?
<--- Score

15. What is an unallowable cost?
<--- Score

16. How will measures be used to manage and adapt?
<--- Score

17. Are there measurements based on task performance?
<--- Score

18. How will you measure success?
<--- Score

19. How is progress measured?
<--- Score

20. How does a lock box-concentration banking system impact a firms float?
<--- Score

21. What evidence is there and what is measured?
<--- Score

22. Have the types of risks that may impact Power purchase agreement been identified and analyzed?
<--- Score

23. Are the units of measure consistent?

<--- Score

24. The approach of traditional Power purchase agreement works for detail complexity but is focused on a systematic approach rather than an understanding of the nature of systems themselves, what approach will permit your organization to deal with the kind of unpredictable emergent behaviors that dynamic complexity can introduce?
<--- Score

25. How will you measure your Power purchase agreement effectiveness?
<--- Score

26. Is Process Variation Displayed/Communicated?
<--- Score

27. Should the chosen fixed-cost rates be actual or budgeted?
<--- Score

28. Do they accurately measure whether you are performing the activity?
<--- Score

29. Is data collection planned and executed?
<--- Score

30. What is our fixed budget for the implementaton and annual costs?
<--- Score

31. How to cause the change?
<--- Score

32. Is the solution cost-effective?
<--- Score

33. Have all non-recommended alternatives been analyzed in sufficient detail?
<--- Score

34. Among the Power purchase agreement product and service cost to be estimated, which is considered hardest to estimate?
<--- Score

35. How large is the gap between current performance and the customer-specified (goal) performance?
<--- Score

36. Is it possible to estimate the impact of unanticipated complexity such as wrong or failed assumptions, feedback, etc. on proposed reforms?
<--- Score

37. What is measured? Why?
<--- Score

38. What are the costs of reform?
<--- Score

39. How is performance measured?
<--- Score

40. Can you measure the return on analysis?
<--- Score

41. Have changes been properly/adequately analyzed for effect?

<--- Score

42. How do you identify and analyze stakeholders and their interests?
<--- Score

43. How do you measure efficient delivery of Power purchase agreement services?
<--- Score

44. What potential environmental factors impact the Power purchase agreement effort?
<--- Score

45. Value Pocket Identification & Quantification: What Are our Value Pockets?
<--- Score

46. Does the Power purchase agreement task fit the client's priorities?
<--- Score

47. How are measurements made?
<--- Score

48. Are the results quantifiable (in terms of percentage of completion)?
<--- Score

49. How will your organization measure success?
<--- Score

50. What are the uncertainties surrounding estimates of impact?
<--- Score

51. Where is it measured?
<--- Score

52. Does the difference between the actual provider costs and the proposed budget exceed 5% on any line item?
<--- Score

53. Do you aggressively reward and promote the people who have the biggest impact on creating excellent Power purchase agreement services/ products?
<--- Score

54. Did you tackle the cause or the symptom?
<--- Score

55. What is the right balance of time and resources between investigation, analysis, and discussion and dissemination?
<--- Score

56. What causes extra work or rework?
<--- Score

57. How can you measure the performance?
<--- Score

58. Can you do Power purchase agreement without complex (expensive) analysis?
<--- Score

59. Is the intent to create a system that will demonstrate that results are being achieved and that results are important, and to focus on best practices by asking, What are you trying to

achieve?
<--- Score

60. What kinds of organizational supports are provided, and how have organizations been changing to accommodate performance measurement?
<--- Score

61. Are losses documented, analyzed, and remedial processes developed to prevent future losses?
<--- Score

62. Does Power purchase agreement analysis isolate the fundamental causes of problems?
<--- Score

63. Which stakeholder characteristics are analyzed?
<--- Score

64. What causes investor action?
<--- Score

65. Ignoring cost differences, are there any advantages of the insurance contract approach versus the use of weather derivatives?
<--- Score

66. What might increase costs beyond the budget?
<--- Score

67. What would be a real cause for concern?
<--- Score

68. What kinds of organizational supports are provided, and how has our oganization

been changing to accommodate performance measurement?
<--- Score

69. How do you focus on what is right -not who is right?
<--- Score

70. Was a data collection plan established?
<--- Score

71. What are the major cost drivers?
<--- Score

72. Does Power purchase agreement analysis show the relationships among important Power purchase agreement factors?
<--- Score

73. Have you made assumptions about the shape of the future, particularly its impact on your customers and competitors?
<--- Score

74. Is data collected on key measures that were identified?
<--- Score

75. What data was collected (past, present, future/ongoing)?
<--- Score

76. How will success or failure be measured?
<--- Score

77. Have you found any 'ground fruit' or 'low-

hanging fruit' for immediate remedies to the gap in performance?
<--- Score

78. Is long term and short term variability accounted for?
<--- Score

79. Who participated in the data collection for measurements?
<--- Score

80. What are the costs for the facility?
<--- Score

81. Is key measure data collection planned and executed, process variation displayed and communicated and performance baselined?
<--- Score

82. How will effects be measured?
<--- Score

83. How do you measure lifecycle phases?
<--- Score

84. Are you taking your company in the direction of better and revenue or cheaper and cost?
<--- Score

85. Is there a Performance Baseline?
<--- Score

86. What intended and expected uses and effects of performance measurement were articulated?
<--- Score

87. What has the team done to assure the stability and accuracy of the measurement process?
<--- Score

88. What particular quality tools did the team find helpful in establishing measurements?
<--- Score

89. Are the measurements objective?
<--- Score

90. Are you aware of what could cause a problem?
<--- Score

91. What causes mismanagement?
<--- Score

92. How can you measure Power purchase agreement in a systematic way?
<--- Score

93. What measurements are possible, practicable and meaningful?
<--- Score

94. How is the value delivered by Power purchase agreement being measured?
<--- Score

95. What are the agreed upon definitions of the high impact areas, defect(s), unit(s), and opportunities that will figure into the process capability metrics?
<--- Score

96. What are the issues and problems caused by

the traditional budgeting approach?
<--- Score

97. Cost – is there a budget?
<--- Score

98. Measured -What are the quantifiable characteristics?
<--- Score

99. Is a solid data collection plan established that includes measurement systems analysis?
<--- Score

100. How do you know that any Power purchase agreement analysis is complete and comprehensive?
<--- Score

101. Are key measures identified and agreed upon?
<--- Score

102. What are the key input variables? What are the key process variables? What are the key output variables?
<--- Score

103. Why do you expend time and effort to implement measurement, for whom?
<--- Score

104. How much does the program cost?
<--- Score

105. What methods are feasible and acceptable to estimate the impact of reforms?
<--- Score

106. Have the concerns of stakeholders to help identify and define potential barriers been obtained and analyzed?
<--- Score

107. What set of input combinations could represent a cost-minimizing choice?
<--- Score

108. For those producers that are successful, the next question that impacts returns is: How long does it take to become successful?
<--- Score

109. What disadvantage does this cause for the user?
<--- Score

110. What specific features of this years budgeting process facilitated consideration of mission and programme priorities?
<--- Score

111. What harm might be caused?
<--- Score

112. Does the company have lower unit costs than its competition?
<--- Score

113. Does Power purchase agreement systematically track and analyze outcomes for accountability and quality improvement?
<--- Score

114. How frequently do you track Power purchase

agreement measures?
<--- Score

115. Are process variation components displayed/ communicated using suitable charts, graphs, plots?
<--- Score

116. How do you measure variability?
<--- Score

117. What are the costs and benefits of maintaining inventories?
<--- Score

118. What are your key Power purchase agreement organizational performance measures, including key short and longer-term financial measures?
<--- Score

119. What key measures identified indicate the performance of the business process?
<--- Score

120. How do you stay flexible and focused to recognize larger Power purchase agreement results?
<--- Score

121. What could cause delays in the schedule?
<--- Score

122. Does your organization systematically track and analyze outcomes related for accountability and quality improvement?
<--- Score

123. What relevant entities could be measured?

<--- Score

124. What are your performance levels and trends for your key measures on student and stakeholder satisfaction and dissatisfaction?
<--- Score

125. What charts has the team used to display the components of variation in the process?
<--- Score

126. Are high impact defects defined and identified in the business process?
<--- Score

127. Can you ensure that vendor turnover will not negatively impact contract performance?
<--- Score

128. Understand the concepts of operating breakeven and financial breakeven. Why is it important to conduct breakeven analyses?
<--- Score

129. How do you do risk analysis of rare, cascading, catastrophic events?
<--- Score

130. Do you effectively measure and reward individual and team performance?
<--- Score

131. How do you control the overall costs of your work processes?
<--- Score

132. What causes innovation to fail or succeed in your organization?
<--- Score

133. Why use opportunity cost?
<--- Score

134. How can the loop be closed between the customer and the supplier, to verify the reliability of the product, if all failures are not documented and reported back to the producer?
<--- Score

135. Do staff have the necessary skills to collect, analyze, and report data?
<--- Score

136. Who should receive measurement reports?
<--- Score

137. Which measures and indicators matter?
<--- Score

138. Who will determine the measures of performance?
<--- Score

139. What are your performance levels for your key measures on budgetary and financial performance, including measures of cost containment, as appropriate?
<--- Score

140. Which error do you think is more likely to occur when firms use payback analysis?
<--- Score

141. What can you predict about future costs?
<--- Score

Add up total points for this section:
_____ = Total points for this section

Divided by: ______ (number of statements answered) = ______ Average score for this section

Transfer your score to the Power purchase agreement Index at the beginning of the Self-Assessment.

CRITERION #4: ANALYZE:

INTENT: Analyze causes, assumptions and hypotheses.

In my belief, the answer to this question is clearly defined:

5 Strongly Agree

4 Agree

3 Neutral

2 Disagree

1 Strongly Disagree

1. What are the revised rough estimates of the financial savings/opportunity for Power purchase agreement improvements?
<--- Score

2. Think about some of the processes you undertake within your organization, which do you own?
<--- Score

3. Think about the functions involved in your Power

purchase agreement project, what processes flow from these functions?
<--- Score

4. What Power purchase agreement data do you gather or use now?
<--- Score

5. Were there any improvement opportunities identified from the process analysis?
<--- Score

6. How we enhance the budget process while addressing long-standing concerns?
<--- Score

7. How do you identify specific Power purchase agreement investment opportunities and emerging trends?
<--- Score

8. How do you implement and manage your work processes to ensure that they meet design requirements?
<--- Score

9. What were the financial benefits resulting from any 'ground fruit or low-hanging fruit' (quick fixes)?
<--- Score

10. Were Pareto charts (or similar) used to portray the 'heavy hitters' (or key sources of variation)?
<--- Score

11. How do you measure the operational performance of your key work systems and processes, including

productivity, cycle time, and other appropriate measures of process effectiveness, efficiency, and innovation?
<--- Score

12. How does the organization define, manage, and improve its Power purchase agreement processes?
<--- Score

13. Do you have documentation you can share about your organizations tool(s) or practices, such as a user manual or an example of tool outputs?
<--- Score

14. Did any additional data need to be collected?
<--- Score

15. A compounding model resolution with available relevant data can often provide insight towards a solution methodology; which Power purchase agreement models, tools and techniques are necessary?
<--- Score

16. Record-keeping requirements flow from the records needed as inputs, outputs, controls and for transformation of a Power purchase agreement process. Are the records needed as inputs to the Power purchase agreement process available?
<--- Score

17. Are Power purchase agreement changes recognized early enough to be approved through the regular process?
<--- Score

18. Do your employees have the opportunity to do what they do best everyday?
<--- Score

19. Where is Power purchase agreement data gathered?
<--- Score

20. Legislature-Driven?
<--- Score

21. What conclusions were drawn from the team's data collection and analysis? How did the team reach these conclusions?
<--- Score

22. Timed -How quickly can it be achieved?
<--- Score

23. What process should you select for improvement?
<--- Score

24. What steps are involved in the capita budgeting process?
<--- Score

25. Is Data and process analysis, root cause analysis and quantifying the gap/opportunity in place?
<--- Score

26. What data is gathered?
<--- Score

27. Do you, as a leader, bounce back quickly from setbacks?
<--- Score

28. What is your organizations process which leads to recognition of value generation?
<--- Score

29. Does a producer have to disclose fees when processing a policy renewal?
<--- Score

30. What controls do you have in place to protect data?
<--- Score

31. Was a detailed process map created to amplify critical steps of the 'as is' business process?
<--- Score

32. What were the crucial 'moments of truth' on the process map?
<--- Score

33. Was a cause-and-effect diagram used to explore the different types of causes (or sources of variation)?
<--- Score

34. What methods do you use to gather Power purchase agreement data?
<--- Score

35. Where is the data coming from to measure compliance?
<--- Score

36. Is the suppliers process defined and controlled?
<--- Score

37. Did any value-added analysis or 'lean thinking' take place to identify some of the gaps shown on the 'as is' process map?
<--- Score

38. What other jobs or tasks affect the performance of the steps in the Power purchase agreement process?
<--- Score

39. What tools were used to narrow the list of possible causes?
<--- Score

40. Have any additional benefits been identified that will result from closing all or most of the gaps?
<--- Score

41. What did the team gain from developing a sub-process map?
<--- Score

42. How was the detailed process map generated, verified, and validated?
<--- Score

43. Is the performance gap determined?
<--- Score

44. What are your key performance measures or indicators and in-process measures for the control and improvement of your Power purchase agreement processes?
<--- Score

45. Is the required Power purchase agreement data gathered?

<--- Score

46. What drives market share?
<--- Score

47. Have the problem and goal statements been updated to reflect the additional knowledge gained from the analyze phase?
<--- Score

48. Can you add value to the current Power purchase agreement decision-making process (largely qualitative) by incorporating uncertainty modeling (more quantitative)?
<--- Score

49. An organizationally feasible system request is one that considers the mission, goals and objectives of the organization. Key questions are: is the Power purchase agreement solution request practical and will it solve a problem or take advantage of an opportunity to achieve company goals?
<--- Score

50. Identify an operational issue in your organization. for example, could a particular task be done more quickly or more efficiently by Power purchase agreement?
<--- Score

51. What provisions should be included in a processing contract for recyclable materials?
<--- Score

52. What are your best practices for minimizing Power purchase agreement project risk, while demonstrating

incremental value and quick wins throughout the Power purchase agreement project lifecycle?
<--- Score

53. How do mission and objectives affect the Power purchase agreement processes of your organization?
<--- Score

54. What are the best opportunities for value improvement?
<--- Score

55. What are your current levels and trends in key Power purchase agreement measures or indicators of product and process performance that are important to and directly serve your customers?
<--- Score

56. Who should be the driver behind implementing the system?
<--- Score

57. What tools were used to generate the list of possible causes?
<--- Score

58. What will drive Power purchase agreement change?
<--- Score

59. What are your current levels and trends in key measures or indicators of Power purchase agreement product and process performance that are important to and directly serve your customers? How do these results compare with the performance of your competitors and other organizations with similar

offerings?
<--- Score

60. How do your work systems and key work processes relate to and capitalize on your core competencies?
<--- Score

61. Is the Power purchase agreement process severely broken such that a re-design is necessary?
<--- Score

62. Do several people in different organizational units assist with the Power purchase agreement process?
<--- Score

63. How is the way you as the leader think and process information affecting your organizational culture?
<--- Score

64. What does the data say about the performance of the business process?
<--- Score

65. How often will data be collected for measures?
<--- Score

66. How is Power purchase agreement data gathered?
<--- Score

67. What other organizational variables, such as reward systems or communication systems, affect the performance of this Power purchase agreement process?
<--- Score

68. Do your contracts/agreements contain data security obligations?
<--- Score

69. What are the six stages of the capital budgeting process?
<--- Score

70. Are gaps between current performance and the goal performance identified?
<--- Score

71. What quality tools were used to get through the analyze phase?
<--- Score

72. How do you promote understanding that opportunity for improvement is not criticism of the status quo, or the people who created the status quo?
<--- Score

73. What are your Power purchase agreement processes?
<--- Score

74. What is the cost of poor quality as supported by the team's analysis?
<--- Score

75. How do you use Power purchase agreement data and information to support organizational decision making and innovation?
<--- Score

76. Were any designed experiments used to generate additional insight into the data analysis?

<--- Score

77. Is the gap/opportunity displayed and communicated in financial terms?
<--- Score

78. Do your leaders quickly bounce back from setbacks?
<--- Score

79. What successful thing are you doing today that may be blinding you to new growth opportunities?
<--- Score

Add up total points for this section:
_____ = Total points for this section

Divided by: ______ (number of statements answered) = ______ Average score for this section

Transfer your score to the Power purchase agreement Index at the beginning of the Self-Assessment.

CRITERION #5: IMPROVE:

INTENT: Develop a practical solution. Innovate, establish and test the solution and to measure the results.

In my belief, the answer to this question is clearly defined:

5 Strongly Agree

4 Agree

3 Neutral

2 Disagree

1 Strongly Disagree

1. How can you improve Power purchase agreement?
<--- Score

2. Did you make a good decision?
<--- Score

3. What can you do to improve?
<--- Score

4. Can the solution be designed and implemented within an acceptable time period?
<--- Score

5. What resources are required for the improvement efforts?
<--- Score

6. How significant is the improvement in the eyes of the end user?
<--- Score

7. What tools were most useful during the improve phase?
<--- Score

8. Are possible solutions generated and tested?
<--- Score

9. An important question is: if a project is undertaken, will failure of the project risk putting the company into bankruptcy?
<--- Score

10. Describe the design of the pilot and what tests were conducted, if any?
<--- Score

11. How will you know when its improved?
<--- Score

12. Have you identified breakpoints and/or risk tolerances that will trigger broad consideration of a potential need for intervention or modification of strategy?
<--- Score

13. What should a proof of concept or pilot accomplish?
<--- Score

14. Are risk triggers captured?
<--- Score

15. What is the Power purchase agreement's sustainability risk?
<--- Score

16. What practices helps your organization to develop its capacity to recognize patterns?
<--- Score

17. What are your performance levels and trends for your key measures and its improvements?
<--- Score

18. What went well, what should change, what can improve?
<--- Score

19. For estimation problems, how do you develop an estimation statement?
<--- Score

20. To what extent does management recognize Power purchase agreement as a tool to increase the results?
<--- Score

21. What communications are necessary to support the implementation of the solution?
<--- Score

22. Who will be responsible for making the decisions to include or exclude requested changes once Power purchase agreement is underway?
<--- Score

23. Understand how we incorporate risk into capital budgeting decisions. What techniques are used?
<--- Score

24. How do the Power purchase agreement results compare with the performance of your competitors and other organizations with similar offerings?
<--- Score

25. Is it optimistic?
<--- Score

26. For decision problems, how do you develop a decision statement?
<--- Score

27. What strategies and initiatives have been developed to meet current and short-term needs?
<--- Score

28. Are new and improved process ('should be') maps developed?
<--- Score

29. How do you keep improving Power purchase agreement?
<--- Score

30. How risky is your organization?

<--- Score

31. Why improve in the first place?
<--- Score

32. Explorations of the frontiers of Power purchase agreement will help you build influence, improve Power purchase agreement, optimize decision making, and sustain change, what is your approach?
<--- Score

33. How do you improve Power purchase agreement service perception, and satisfaction?
<--- Score

34. Is a contingency plan established?
<--- Score

35. What to do with the results or outcomes of measurements?
<--- Score

36. Do Managerial Motives Influence Firm Risk Reduction Strategies?
<--- Score

37. Is there a small-scale pilot for proposed improvement(s)? What conclusions were drawn from the outcomes of a pilot?
<--- Score

38. Are improved process ('should be') maps modified based on pilot data and analysis?
<--- Score

39. Who will be responsible for documenting the

Power purchase agreement requirements in detail?
<--- Score

40. Is the measure of success for Power purchase agreement understandable to a variety of people?
<--- Score

41. In the past few months, what is the smallest change you have made that has had the biggest positive result? What was it about that small change that produced the large return?
<--- Score

42. How do you decide how much to remunerate an employee?
<--- Score

43. What might the legislature do in setting policy to improve the outcomes of the program?
<--- Score

44. How will you know that you have improved?
<--- Score

45. What tools were used to evaluate the potential solutions?
<--- Score

46. How can poor capital budgeting decisions produce negative effects to the firm?
<--- Score

47. Are you assessing Power purchase agreement and risk?
<--- Score

48. How will the organization know that the solution worked?
<--- Score

49. Are risks identified?
<--- Score

50. Who are the people involved in developing and implementing Power purchase agreement?
<--- Score

51. What improvements have been achieved?
<--- Score

52. Risk factors: what are the characteristics of Power purchase agreement that make it risky?
<--- Score

53. Can you identify any significant risks or exposures to Power purchase agreement third- parties (vendors, service providers, alliance partners etc) that concern you?
<--- Score

54. What are the implications of the one critical Power purchase agreement decision 10 minutes, 10 months, and 10 years from now?
<--- Score

55. Were any criteria developed to assist the team in testing and evaluating potential solutions?
<--- Score

56. Is there a high likelihood that any recommendations will achieve their intended results?
<--- Score

57. Understand what an NPV profile is, how it is used, and how it is constructed?
<--- Score

58. How do you link measurement and risk?
<--- Score

59. Is the solution technically practical?
<--- Score

60. Can we continue to improve and create value?
<--- Score

61. What is the team's contingency plan for potential problems occurring in implementation?
<--- Score

62. What do you hope to achieve as a result of your communications activities?
<--- Score

63. What is Power purchase agreement's impact on utilizing the best solution(s)?
<--- Score

64. What is the magnitude of the improvements?
<--- Score

65. Who makes the purchasing decision?
<--- Score

66. What attendant changes will need to be made to ensure that the solution is successful?
<--- Score

67. Are there any constraints (technical, political, cultural, or otherwise) that would inhibit certain solutions?
<--- Score

68. How does the team improve its work?
<--- Score

69. How did the team generate the list of possible solutions?
<--- Score

70. Are the best solutions selected?
<--- Score

71. What error proofing will be done to address some of the discrepancies observed in the 'as is' process?
<--- Score

72. Who controls key decisions that will be made?
<--- Score

73. How can you improve performance?
<--- Score

74. Is the optimal solution selected based on testing and analysis?
<--- Score

75. What lessons, if any, from a pilot were incorporated into the design of the full-scale solution?
<--- Score

76. What are the various types of capital budgeting decisions?
<--- Score

77. Is pilot data collected and analyzed?
<--- Score

78. Under what circumstances will the NPV, IRR, and PI techniques provide different capital budgeting decisions?
<--- Score

79. What do you want to improve?
<--- Score

80. Is there a cost/benefit analysis of optimal solution(s)?
<--- Score

81. Achievable -Can you improve on past performance?
<--- Score

82. How will you know that a change is an improvement?
<--- Score

83. How do we choose among the methods for evaluating capital investments?
<--- Score

84. Who will be using the results of the measurement activities?
<--- Score

85. Who controls the risk?
<--- Score

86. Are there contractual recourses that the

organization can take if a third-party developer delivers software that contains malicious code?
<--- Score

87. If you could go back in time five years, what decision would you make differently? What is your best guess as to what decision you're making today you might regret five years from now?
<--- Score

88. Is the implementation plan designed?
<--- Score

89. How do you measure risk?
<--- Score

90. When a producer evaluates the list of the tasks required to complete a production, the first question he or she should ask is How long will it take to reasonably complete this task?
<--- Score

91. Risk Identification: What are the possible risk events your organization faces in relation to Power purchase agreement?
<--- Score

92. Do you combine technical expertise with business knowledge and Power purchase agreement Key topics include lifecycles, development approaches, requirements and how to make a business case?
<--- Score

93. Why are capital budgeting decisions important to the success of a firm?
<--- Score

94. How is the WACC used to make capital budgeting decisions?
<--- Score

95. If there exists an optimal level of self-imposed exit restrictions, is there an adoption of a unique contract with these characteristics?
<--- Score

96. Have you developed an overall project budget?
<--- Score

97. Does the goal represent a desired result that can be measured?
<--- Score

98. Is the scope clearly documented?
<--- Score

99. Business risk -will vendor deliver as contracted?
<--- Score

100. How will you measure the results?
<--- Score

101. Is a solution implementation plan established, including schedule/work breakdown structure, resources, risk management plan, cost/budget, and control plan?
<--- Score

102. What actually has to improve and by how much?
<--- Score

103. How can good capital budgeting decisions increase the value of a firm?
<--- Score

104. Is supporting Power purchase agreement documentation required?
<--- Score

105. What are your current levels and trends in key measures or indicators of workforce and leader development?
<--- Score

106. How do you manage and improve your Power purchase agreement work systems to deliver customer value and achieve organizational success and sustainability?
<--- Score

107. How do you measure improved Power purchase agreement service perception, and satisfaction?
<--- Score

108. Risk events: what are the things that could go wrong?
<--- Score

109. Who has been involved in initiating, developing, and using performance measurement, and how have they been involved?
<--- Score

110. How do you define the solutions' scope?
<--- Score

111. How do you measure progress and evaluate

training effectiveness?
<--- Score

112. What is the implementation plan?
<--- Score

113. How do you improve your likelihood of success ?
<--- Score

114. How will the team or the process owner(s) monitor the implementation plan to see that it is working as intended?
<--- Score

115. What tools do you use once you have decided on a Power purchase agreement strategy and more importantly how do you choose?
<--- Score

116. What are the results?
<--- Score

117. Can contractor accurately reevaluate problems on a job?
<--- Score

118. What does the 'should be' process map/design look like?
<--- Score

119. At what point will vulnerability assessments be performed once Power purchase agreement is put into production (e.g., ongoing Risk Management after implementation)?
<--- Score

120. Is it mandatory to transfer all physical documents in digital format? If I have a physical contract for example; do I a have to put it in digital format?
<--- Score

121. What needs improvement? Why?
<--- Score

122. How does the solution remove the key sources of issues discovered in the analyze phase?
<--- Score

123. How do you go about comparing Power purchase agreement approaches/solutions?
<--- Score

124. Do those selected for the Power purchase agreement team have a good general understanding of what Power purchase agreement is all about?
<--- Score

125. How can skill-level changes improve Power purchase agreement?
<--- Score

126. Was a pilot designed for the proposed solution(s)?
<--- Score

127. What is the risk?
<--- Score

128. Will the controls trigger any other risks?
<--- Score

129. How do you improve productivity?
<--- Score

130. Which of the recognised risks out of all risks can be most likely transferred?
<--- Score

131. Are there diminishing returns to risk taking?
<--- Score

132. What tools were used to tap into the creativity and encourage 'outside the box' thinking?
<--- Score

133. Contractor Workers – Are contractors safety and health programs and performance (including rates) evaluated?
<--- Score

134. What were the underlying assumptions on the cost-benefit analysis?
<--- Score

Add up total points for this section:
_____ = Total points for this section

Divided by: ______ (number of statements answered) = ______
Average score for this section

Transfer your score to the Power purchase agreement Index at the beginning of the Self-Assessment.

CRITERION #6: CONTROL:

INTENT: Implement the practical solution. Maintain the performance and correct possible complications.

In my belief, the answer to this question is clearly defined:

5 Strongly Agree

4 Agree

3 Neutral

2 Disagree

1 Strongly Disagree

1. Can support from partners be adjusted?
<--- Score

2. Is reporting being used or needed?
<--- Score

3. What lessons have been learned from the performance measurement experience to date, and what are future expectations for the use of

performance measurement?
<--- Score

4. What are our organisational objectives this financial year and to what extent are these reflected in our current budget?
<--- Score

5. How does your division/department/committee/office plan to meet a growing demand for services?
<--- Score

6. What are the known security controls?
<--- Score

7. What are the critical parameters to watch?
<--- Score

8. What other systems, operations, processes, and infrastructures (hiring practices, staffing, training, incentives/rewards, metrics/dashboards/scorecards, etc.) need updates, additions, changes, or deletions in order to facilitate knowledge transfer and improvements?
<--- Score

9. How will the process owner verify improvement in present and future sigma levels, process capabilities?
<--- Score

10. Are there documented procedures?
<--- Score

11. What is the optimal detailed activity plan for the final, actual allocation?
<--- Score

12. What are your results for key measures or indicators of the accomplishment of your Power purchase agreement strategy and action plans, including building and strengthening core competencies?
<--- Score

13. How can you best use all of your knowledge repositories to enhance learning and sharing?
<--- Score

14. How might the organization capture best practices and lessons learned so as to leverage improvements across the business?
<--- Score

15. Will your goals reflect your program budget?
<--- Score

16. Is the standard deviation of the stock equal to the standard deviation of the market?
<--- Score

17. Who has control over resources?
<--- Score

18. Is there documentation that will support the successful operation of the improvement?
<--- Score

19. Does job training on the documented procedures need to be part of the process team's education and training?
<--- Score

20. How will you measure your QA plan's effectiveness?
<--- Score

21. How will new or emerging customer needs/ requirements be checked/communicated to orient the process toward meeting the new specifications and continually reducing variation?
<--- Score

22. How will the day-to-day responsibilities for monitoring and continual improvement be transferred from the improvement team to the process owner?
<--- Score

23. Has the improved process and its steps been standardized?
<--- Score

24. How likely is the current Power purchase agreement plan to come in on schedule or on budget?
<--- Score

25. You may have created your quality measures at a time when you lacked resources, technology wasn't up to the required standard, or low service levels were the industry norm. Have those circumstances changed?
<--- Score

26. Is there a control plan in place for sustaining improvements (short and long-term)?
<--- Score

27. What should the next improvement project be that is related to Power purchase agreement?
<--- Score

28. Screening decisions. Does a proposed project meet some preset standard of acceptance?
<--- Score

29. When using the time adjusted rate of return method, how does one know when the true rate of return has been found?
<--- Score

30. Is there a transfer of ownership and knowledge to process owner and process team tasked with the responsibilities.
<--- Score

31. Where do ideas that reach policy makers and planners as proposals for Power purchase agreement strengthening and reform actually originate?
<--- Score

32. What do your reports reflect?
<--- Score

33. Is there a documented and implemented monitoring plan?
<--- Score

34. Is there a Power purchase agreement Communication plan covering who needs to get what information when?
<--- Score

35. What can you control?

<--- Score

36. How do you plan on providing proper recognition and disclosure of supporting companies?
<--- Score

37. What is the control/monitoring plan?
<--- Score

38. What is the best design framework for Power purchase agreement organization now that, in a post industrial-age if the top-down, command and control model is no longer relevant?
<--- Score

39. Does Power purchase agreement appropriately measure and monitor risk?
<--- Score

40. Can you adapt and adjust to changing Power purchase agreement situations?
<--- Score

41. What quality tools were useful in the control phase?
<--- Score

42. What key inputs and outputs are being measured on an ongoing basis?
<--- Score

43. Implementation Planning: is a pilot needed to test the changes before a full roll out occurs?
<--- Score

44. What is the recommended frequency of auditing?

<--- Score

45. Does the response plan contain a definite closed loop continual improvement scheme (e.g., plan-do-check-act)?
<--- Score

46. Have new or revised work instructions resulted?
<--- Score

47. How will the process owner and team be able to hold the gains?
<--- Score

48. What should you measure to verify efficiency gains?
<--- Score

49. Are the planned controls in place?
<--- Score

50. What do you stand for--and what are you against?
<--- Score

51. Do the Power purchase agreement decisions you make today help people and the planet tomorrow?
<--- Score

52. Whether youre preparing a 12, 24 or 36 month communications plan, what tools will you need to use during this timeframe?
<--- Score

53. Do you monitor the Power purchase agreement decisions made and fine tune them as they evolve?
<--- Score

54. What is your theory of human motivation, and how does your compensation plan fit with that view?
<--- Score

55. How do your controls stack up?
<--- Score

56. Who is the Power purchase agreement process owner?
<--- Score

57. What are you attempting to measure/monitor?
<--- Score

58. How do you select, collect, align, and integrate Power purchase agreement data and information for tracking daily operations and overall organizational performance, including progress relative to strategic objectives and action plans?
<--- Score

59. Does a troubleshooting guide exist or is it needed?
<--- Score

60. Who sets the Power purchase agreement standards?
<--- Score

61. Is a response plan established and deployed?
<--- Score

62. How do you encourage people to take control and responsibility?
<--- Score

63. How do we control for cannibalization w/ other channels (direct)?
<--- Score

64. Act/Adjust: What Do you Need to Do Differently?
<--- Score

65. Will the team be available to assist members in planning investigations?
<--- Score

66. How do you establish and deploy modified action plans if circumstances require a shift in plans and rapid execution of new plans?
<--- Score

67. Are suggested corrective/restorative actions indicated on the response plan for known causes to problems that might surface?
<--- Score

68. How much or how well has your division/ department/committee/office accomplished or implemented each part of its plan?
<--- Score

69. In the case of a Power purchase agreement project, the criteria for the audit derive from implementation objectives. an audit of a Power purchase agreement project involves assessing whether the recommendations outlined for implementation have been met. Can you track that any Power purchase agreement project is implemented as planned, and is it working?
<--- Score

70. If no risks are offered, is there an explanation of which risks were evaluated or considered and how they were mitigated?
<--- Score

71. Are operating procedures consistent?
<--- Score

72. What other areas of the organization might benefit from the Power purchase agreement team's improvements, knowledge, and learning?
<--- Score

73. Who will be in control?
<--- Score

74. How do controls support value?
<--- Score

75. Is a response plan in place for when the input, process, or output measures indicate an 'out-of-control' condition?
<--- Score

76. Is knowledge gained on process shared and institutionalized?
<--- Score

77. Do you monitor the effectiveness of your Power purchase agreement activities?
<--- Score

78. How is change control managed?
<--- Score

79. Is there a recommended audit plan for routine

surveillance inspections of Power purchase agreement's gains?
<--- Score

80. Are new process steps, standards, and documentation ingrained into normal operations?
<--- Score

81. Have the factors limiting ability to accomplish or implement any part of the plan been identified (finances, time, training, physical space, equipment, etc.)?
<--- Score

82. Will any special training be provided for results interpretation?
<--- Score

83. How will report readings be checked to effectively monitor performance?
<--- Score

84. Does the Power purchase agreement performance meet the customer's requirements?
<--- Score

85. Are you measuring, monitoring and predicting Power purchase agreement activities to optimize operations and profitability, and enhancing outcomes?
<--- Score

86. How do senior leaders actions reflect a commitment to the organizations Power purchase agreement values?
<--- Score

87. Are controls in place and consistently applied?
<--- Score

88. Who controls critical resources?
<--- Score

89. What adjustments to the strategies are needed?
<--- Score

90. What are the key elements of your Power purchase agreement performance improvement system, including your evaluation, organizational learning, and innovation processes?
<--- Score

91. Against what alternative is success being measured?
<--- Score

92. Is new knowledge gained imbedded in the response plan?
<--- Score

93. What do you measure to verify effectiveness gains?
<--- Score

94. Are documented procedures clear and easy to follow for the operators?
<--- Score

95. Are pertinent alerts monitored, analyzed and distributed to appropriate personnel?
<--- Score

96. Is there a standardized process?
<--- Score

97. Are the planned controls working?
<--- Score

98. How will input, process, and output variables be checked to detect for sub-optimal conditions?
<--- Score

Add up total points for this section:
_____ = Total points for this section

Divided by: ______ (number of statements answered) = ______
Average score for this section

Transfer your score to the Power purchase agreement Index at the beginning of the Self-Assessment.

CRITERION #7: SUSTAIN:

INTENT: Retain the benefits.

In my belief, the answer to this question is clearly defined:

5 Strongly Agree

4 Agree

3 Neutral

2 Disagree

1 Strongly Disagree

1. What is the source of the strategies for Power purchase agreement strengthening and reform?
<--- Score

2. Engagement letter. did the audit contract, engagement letter, or agreement include the following?
<--- Score

3. Did you reach the right audience?
<--- Score

4. Is Power purchase agreement dependent on the successful delivery of a current project?
<--- Score

5. What does your signature ensure?
<--- Score

6. How do you ensure that implementations of Power purchase agreement products are done in a way that ensures safety?
<--- Score

7. If vendor is unwilling to address your concerns, can you modify or exit the contract?
<--- Score

8. If private, does the facility manager want the projects assets on or off the balance sheet?
<--- Score

9. What are the potential basics of Power purchase agreement fraud?
<--- Score

10. If other test accuracy ratios less than 4 to 1 are maintained or are they limited by the state of the art or allowed by contract?
<--- Score

11. Are there any disadvantages to implementing Power purchase agreement? There might be some that are less obvious?
<--- Score

12. If no one would ever find out about your

accomplishments, how would you lead differently?
<--- Score

13. Will I be able to upgrade to another contract?
<--- Score

14. Are the criteria for selecting recommendations stated?
<--- Score

15. How do you lead with Power purchase agreement in mind?
<--- Score

16. How do you create buy-in?
<--- Score

17. Is there a timeline offered for when benefits will be realized?
<--- Score

18. Does it challenge?
<--- Score

19. Exclusivity – Are you contractually bound to just one ACO?
<--- Score

20. What did you miss in the interview for the worst hire you ever made?
<--- Score

21. How do you stay inspired?
<--- Score

22. What is the craziest thing you can do?

<--- Score

23. What are specific Power purchase agreement rules to follow?
<--- Score

24. Think of your Power purchase agreement project, what are the main functions?
<--- Score

25. Are you relevant? Will you be relevant five years from now? Ten?
<--- Score

26. Who do you think the world wants your organization to be?
<--- Score

27. What changes produce new financial regulations?
<--- Score

28. What is effective Power purchase agreement?
<--- Score

29. What are you challenging?
<--- Score

30. What is Internal Rate of Return (IRR)?
<--- Score

31. Are you / should you be revolutionary or evolutionary?
<--- Score

32. Do you have the right capabilities and capacities?

<--- Score

33. Is your basic point _____ or _____?
<--- Score

34. When was the last time you reviewed the level of reserves in relation to our annual operating budget?
<--- Score

35. What are the business goals Power purchase agreement is aiming to achieve?
<--- Score

36. How do you foster innovation?
<--- Score

37. Are there any advantages of the insurance contract approach versus the use of the weather derivatives?
<--- Score

38. Who have you, as a company, historically been when you've been at your best?
<--- Score

39. What is the funding source for this project?
<--- Score

40. How much does Power purchase agreement help?
<--- Score

41. What are the success criteria that will indicate that Power purchase agreement objectives have been met and the benefits delivered?
<--- Score

42. Can you break it down?
<--- Score

43. Whose voice (department, ethnic group, women, older workers, etc) might you have missed hearing from in your company, and how might you amplify this voice to create positive momentum for your business?
<--- Score

44. Why should people listen to you?
<--- Score

45. Are these laboratories on an approved subcontractor list?
<--- Score

46. What are internal and external Power purchase agreement relations?
<--- Score

47. How do we budget and why?
<--- Score

48. When you map the key players in your own work and the types/domains of relationships with them, which relationships do you find easy and which challenging, and why?
<--- Score

49. What are the key enablers to make this Power purchase agreement move?
<--- Score

50. How will you motivate the stakeholders with the

least vested interest?
<--- Score

51. What happens at your organization when people fail?
<--- Score

52. How to intervene?
<--- Score

53. Have new benefits been realized?
<--- Score

54. What are your personal philosophies regarding Power purchase agreement and how do they influence your work?
<--- Score

55. What is Extended Producer Responsibility?
<--- Score

56. What are the long-term Power purchase agreement goals?
<--- Score

57. What may be the consequences for the performance of an organization if all stakeholders are not consulted regarding Power purchase agreement?
<--- Score

58. What are the primary distinctions between foreign capital investments and domestic investments?
<--- Score

59. Why is Power purchase agreement important for

you now?
<--- Score

60. What are our own strengths and weaknesses?
<--- Score

61. How are you doing compared to your industry?
<--- Score

62. Have benefits been optimized with all key stakeholders?
<--- Score

63. How can you become more high-tech but still be high touch?
<--- Score

64. How do we look to shareholders?
<--- Score

65. Did your employees make progress today?
<--- Score

66. What is the IRR?
<--- Score

67. How is implementation research currently incorporated into each of your goals?
<--- Score

68. How do you make it meaningful in connecting Power purchase agreement with what users do day-to-day?
<--- Score

69. What should you stop doing?

<--- Score

70. How will you know that the Power purchase agreement project has been successful?
<--- Score

71. Whom among your colleagues do you trust, and for what?
<--- Score

72. Who is responsible for Power purchase agreement?
<--- Score

73. What management system can you use to leverage the Power purchase agreement experience, ideas, and concerns of the people closest to the work to be done?
<--- Score

74. Are new benefits received and understood?
<--- Score

75. How Many Metrics Are Used?
<--- Score

76. Informative or Determinative?
<--- Score

77. What is your Power purchase agreement strategy?
<--- Score

78. How should we establish our marketing communications budget?
<--- Score

79. How do you govern and fulfill your societal responsibilities?
<--- Score

80. Would you rather sell to knowledgeable and informed customers or to uninformed customers?
<--- Score

81. What successes have you experienced in utilizing performance-based budgeting?
<--- Score

82. Which individuals, teams or departments will be involved in Power purchase agreement?
<--- Score

83. What factors affect progress?
<--- Score

84. Is there any existing Power purchase agreement governance structure?
<--- Score

85. What are strategies for increasing support and reducing opposition?
<--- Score

86. Are there instances where you spend more than was on the original contract?
<--- Score

87. Instead of going to current contacts for new ideas, what if you reconnected with dormant contacts--the people you used to know? If you were going reactivate a dormant tie, who would it be?
<--- Score

88. What techniques are used?
<--- Score

89. What have been your experiences in defining long range Power purchase agreement goals?
<--- Score

90. What is your competitive advantage?
<--- Score

91. Is a Power purchase agreement team work effort in place?
<--- Score

92. What is capital budgeting?
<--- Score

93. What is DCF technique Capital Budgeting?
<--- Score

94. What would you recommend your friend do if he/she were facing this dilemma?
<--- Score

95. Are you satisfied with your current role? If not, what is missing from it?
<--- Score

96. How will you know if you have succeeded and met your objectives?
<--- Score

97. Is there any reason to believe the opposite of my current belief?
<--- Score

98. Ask yourself: how would you do this work if you only had one staff member to do it?
<--- Score

99. Who else should you help?
<--- Score

100. Are there any dangers of this system that you can envisage?
<--- Score

101. Are the assumptions believable and achievable?
<--- Score

102. Have we provided written notification to our lower-tier subrecipients regarding their responsibilities to be alert for instances of fraud, abuse, and criminal activity committed by staff, contractors, or program participants and to report all such instances immediately?
<--- Score

103. If you find that you havent accomplished one of the goals for one of the steps of the Power purchase agreement strategy, what will you do to fix it?
<--- Score

104. What current systems have to be understood and/or changed?
<--- Score

105. Where can you break convention?
<--- Score

106. What unique value proposition (UVP) do you

offer?
<--- Score

107. What Types of Initial Training are Provided and How Many Types of Training are Provided to to Young Producers?
<--- Score

108. What does the IRS use for its depreciable basis guidelines?
<--- Score

109. How likely is it that a customer would recommend your company to a friend or colleague?
<--- Score

110. Does your organization utilize performance-based budgeting to allocate funds associated with maintenance activities?
<--- Score

111. How is EPB different than OFA/OSA?
<--- Score

112. What potential megatrends could make your business model obsolete?
<--- Score

113. Will it be accepted by users?
<--- Score

114. What is the estimated value of the project?
<--- Score

115. What Power purchase agreement modifications can you make work for you?

<--- Score

116. In what way is the NPV consistent with the principle of shareholder wealth maximization?
<--- Score

117. How can you incorporate support to ensure safe and effective use of Power purchase agreement into the services that you provide?
<--- Score

118. What margin do we give?
<--- Score

119. How do other organizations budget?
<--- Score

120. Is the impact that Power purchase agreement has shown?
<--- Score

121. What would have to be true for the option on the table to be the best possible choice?
<--- Score

122. Defining PBB Who, What, Where, When?
<--- Score

123. Is there a contract for a set period, or is there a month-on-month ongoing contract?
<--- Score

124. What is operating leverage?
<--- Score

125. Why do and why don't your customers like your

organization?
<--- Score

126. Are Young Producers Generalists or Who Manages Young Producers?
<--- Score

127. Do you have enough freaky customers in your portfolio pushing you to the limit day in and day out?
<--- Score

128. What is a feasible sequencing of reform initiatives over time?
<--- Score

129. What happens on vendor contract renewal and material change?
<--- Score

130. Producer push or consumer pull?
<--- Score

131. Does the calibration lab or calibration contractor provide the end user notification of any out of tolerance conditions?
<--- Score

132. Do you feel that more should be done in the Power purchase agreement area?
<--- Score

133. If you were responsible for initiating and implementing major changes in your organization, what steps might you take to ensure acceptance of those changes?
<--- Score

134. How can you negotiate Power purchase agreement successfully with a stubborn boss, an irate client, or a deceitful coworker?
<--- Score

135. If you had to leave your organization for a year and the only communication you could have with employees/colleagues was a single paragraph, what would you write?
<--- Score

136. Are your responses positive or negative?
<--- Score

137. What products should the firm sell?
<--- Score

138. At what point must a producer disclose fees to a consumer?
<--- Score

139. Who do we want your customers to become?
<--- Score

140. How important is Power purchase agreement to the user organizations mission?
<--- Score

141. What is your formula for success in Power purchase agreement ?
<--- Score

142. How do you deal with Power purchase agreement changes?
<--- Score

143. To whom do you add value?
<--- Score

144. Why stewardship programs?
<--- Score

145. What you are going to do to affect the numbers?
<--- Score

146. How intense is the competition?
<--- Score

147. Who Pays for the Internet?
<--- Score

148. What happens when a new employee joins the organization?
<--- Score

149. Who will determine interim and final deadlines?
<--- Score

150. Does the product fit into the current product mix?
<--- Score

151. At the point of contract renewal, how will vendors be treated?
<--- Score

152. What are the essentials of internal Power purchase agreement management?
<--- Score

153. Are you using a design thinking approach and

integrating Innovation, Power purchase agreement Experience, and Brand Value?
<--- Score

154. In retrospect, of the projects that you pulled the plug on, what percent do you wish had been allowed to keep going, and what percent do you wish had ended earlier?
<--- Score

155. What are the short and long-term Power purchase agreement goals?
<--- Score

156. What new services of functionality will be implemented next with Power purchase agreement ?
<--- Score

157. Should we use performance-based budgeting?
<--- Score

158. What Power purchase agreement skills are most important?
<--- Score

159. Do you see more potential in people than they do in themselves?
<--- Score

160. What are our own strengths and weaknesses?
<--- Score

161. How do you cross-sell and up-sell your Power purchase agreement success?
<--- Score

162. Do you have an implicit bias for capital investments over people investments?
<--- Score

163. What must a general contractor do to correct health and safety violations and enforce health and safety rules?
<--- Score

164. Budgets and resources have been allocated
<--- Score

165. How much value has the business created in the year?
<--- Score

166. Balance of internal versus external labor: what is a healthy balance in budget for external hiring versus staffing the organization?
<--- Score

167. How do you accomplish your long range Power purchase agreement goals?
<--- Score

168. Using the discounted payback rule, should the firm invest in the new product?
<--- Score

169. Is it persevering?
<--- Score

170. How do you set Power purchase agreement stretch targets and how do you get people to not only participate in setting these stretch targets but also

that they strive to achieve these?
<--- Score

171. Is a separate bank account maintained for grant/contract funds?
<--- Score

172. When using the net present value method, how does one know whether the true rate of return is greater or less than the discount rate?
<--- Score

173. Is maximizing Power purchase agreement protection the same as minimizing Power purchase agreement loss?
<--- Score

174. Is the true rate of return greater than or less than the discount rate?
<--- Score

175. What one word do you want to own in the minds of your customers, employees, and partners?
<--- Score

176. Were lessons learned captured and communicated?
<--- Score

177. It is difficult to know if youve got the right spending level. however, the agency should provide a range of budgets for the products they advertise. how much does the top advertiser spend?
<--- Score

178. How are allocations determined with reduced funding?
<--- Score

179. What is Product Stewardship and Extended Producer Responsibility (EPR)?
<--- Score

180. If you had to rebuild your organization without any traditional competitive advantages (i.e., no killer a technology, promising research, innovative product/ service delivery model, etc.), how would your people have to approach their work and collaborate together in order to create the necessary conditions for success?
<--- Score

181. Are you paying enough attention to the partners your company depends on to succeed?
<--- Score

182. What business benefits will Power purchase agreement goals deliver if achieved?
<--- Score

183. How do you manage Power purchase agreement Knowledge Management (KM)?
<--- Score

184. What is one break point that a firm always faces?
<--- Score

185. Is it economical; do you have the time and money?
<--- Score

186. What role does communication play in the success or failure of a Power purchase agreement project?
<--- Score

187. How do you proactively clarify deliverables and Power purchase agreement quality expectations?
<--- Score

188. How does Power purchase agreement integrate with other business initiatives?
<--- Score

189. What is the recommended frequency of auditing?
<--- Score

190. How do shareholders get returns?
<--- Score

191. Who is on the team?
<--- Score

192. Are you maintaining a past–present–future perspective throughout the Power purchase agreement discussion?
<--- Score

193. Do you know what you are doing? And who do you call if you don't?
<--- Score

194. Does the project comply with all rules and regulations?
<--- Score

195. Is it credible?
<--- Score

196. Can you do all this work?
<--- Score

197. What will it take in order to get from current levels of performance to that level specified in the objectives?
<--- Score

198. What trophy do you want on your mantle?
<--- Score

199. How do you go about securing Power purchase agreement?
<--- Score

200. How much contingency will be available in the budget?
<--- Score

201. Why change, why now?
<--- Score

202. Can you Predict the Future?
<--- Score

203. What are the major weaknesses of the payback method?
<--- Score

204. Have you ever been over budget?
<--- Score

205. What is the annual or total budget for this

project?
<--- Score

206. What does the stock sell for today?
<--- Score

207. How do you provide a safe environment -physically and emotionally?
<--- Score

208. If there were zero limitations, what would you do differently?
<--- Score

209. At what moment would you think; Will I get fired?
<--- Score

210. Who is responsible for ensuring appropriate resources (time, people and money) are allocated to Power purchase agreement?
<--- Score

211. Do you say no to customers for no reason?
<--- Score

212. What is your BATNA (best alternative to a negotiated agreement)?
<--- Score

213. Which models, tools and techniques are necessary?
<--- Score

214. What are your most important goals for the strategic Power purchase agreement objectives?
<--- Score

215. How Are Metrics Selected?
<--- Score

216. Can you maintain your growth without detracting from the factors that have contributed to your success?
<--- Score

217. What are some useful resources for recyclable materials contracting?
<--- Score

218. What are the rules and assumptions your industry operates under? What if the opposite were true?
<--- Score

219. Have significant deviations between realised income and expenses and the approved budget been explained?
<--- Score

220. What type of products would work well under a dynamic pricing model?
<--- Score

221. How will you ensure you get what you expected?
<--- Score

222. What counts that you are not counting?
<--- Score

223. When can a producer charge a service fee?
<--- Score

224. Do you think Power purchase agreement

accomplishes the goals you expect it to accomplish?
<--- Score

225. Do you think you know, or do you know you know ?
<--- Score

226. Who is accountable for which actions?
<--- Score

227. What knowledge, skills and characteristics mark a good Power purchase agreement project manager?
<--- Score

228. What is the investments payback period?
<--- Score

229. Hourly rates billed to contract maximums?
<--- Score

230. How has it changed over time and where is it headed in the future?
<--- Score

231. Why is it important to have senior management support for a Power purchase agreement project?
<--- Score

232. What is something you believe that nearly no one agrees with you on?
<--- Score

233. Which departments arent using the preferred/ contracted supplier in a given category?
<--- Score

234. Is the Power purchase agreement organization completing tasks effectively and efficiently?
<--- Score

235. What goals did you miss?
<--- Score

236. Time management is perhaps the most fundamental aspect of being a producer. Indeed, time management is the single biggest factor that affects whether a production is cancelled. Why?
<--- Score

237. Is Power purchase agreement realistic, or are you setting yourself up for failure?
<--- Score

238. Who pays for IT?
<--- Score

239. Who are your customers?
<--- Score

240. Who do you want your customers to become?
<--- Score

241. What do we do when new problems arise?
<--- Score

242. Does the vendor reside entirely within your country, including subcontractors?
<--- Score

243. Why is it so hard to change traditional budgeting methods?
<--- Score

244. How do you transition from the baseline to the target?
<--- Score

245. What is requested from the Board?
<--- Score

246. What was the last experiment you ran?
<--- Score

247. In a project to restructure Power purchase agreement outcomes, which stakeholders would you involve?
<--- Score

248. What markets should the firm be in?
<--- Score

249. How do you keep records, of what?
<--- Score

250. How do you determine the key elements that affect Power purchase agreement workforce satisfaction, how are these elements determined for different workforce groups and segments?
<--- Score

251. Which investments does the firm accept if the cutoff payback period is three years?
<--- Score

252. Operational - will it work?
<--- Score

253. What are the challenges?

<--- Score

254. If you weren't already in this business, would you enter it today? And if not, what are you going to do about it?
<--- Score

255. What new products should the firm introduce?
<--- Score

256. Who uses your product in ways you never expected?
<--- Score

257. Are there any activities that you can take off your to do list?
<--- Score

258. What are the potential faults in using the IRR as a capital budgeting technique?
<--- Score

259. How will the finance function within business change over the next five years?
<--- Score

260. Marketing budgets are tighter, consumers are more skeptical, and social media has changed forever the way we talk about Power purchase agreement. How do you gain traction?
<--- Score

261. What are the yearly depreciation allowances using ACRS depreciation?
<--- Score

262. Which functions and people interact with the supplier and or customer?
<--- Score

263. What is the basic present value equation used in capital budgeting?
<--- Score

264. What industries should the firm be in?
<--- Score

265. Which Power purchase agreement goals are the most important?
<--- Score

266. Will my recycling program make money?
<--- Score

267. What is the kind of project structure that would be appropriate for your Power purchase agreement project, should it be formal and complex, or can it be less formal and relatively simple?
<--- Score

268. What are current Power purchase agreement paradigms?
<--- Score

269. Are these strategies and initiatives current, comprehensive, and properly stated?
<--- Score

270. Do we have the financial resources available?
<--- Score

271. If two investments have the same payback period, are they equally desirable?
<--- Score

272. How will you insure seamless interoperability of Power purchase agreement moving forward?
<--- Score

273. How do you know if you are successful?
<--- Score

274. What will be the consequences to the stakeholder (financial, reputation etc) if Power purchase agreement does not go ahead or fails to deliver the objectives?
<--- Score

275. What is an unauthorized commitment?
<--- Score

276. When information truly is ubiquitous, when reach and connectivity are completely global, when computing resources are infinite, and when a whole new set of impossibilities are not only possible, but happening, what will that do to your business?
<--- Score

277. Will there be any necessary staff changes (redundancies or new hires)?
<--- Score

278. What have you invested?
<--- Score

279. What are you trying to prove to yourself, and how might it be hijacking your life and business success?

<--- Score

280. What actions should corporate managers take before implementing a project?
<--- Score

281. How do you come up with the right discounted payback period cut-off?
<--- Score

282. What is the range of capabilities?
<--- Score

283. Do you have past Power purchase agreement successes?
<--- Score

284. In which businesses should the firm invest money?
<--- Score

285. If your company went out of business tomorrow, would anyone who doesn't get a paycheck here care?
<--- Score

286. What are the major barriers to implementing these changes?
<--- Score

287. Why not do Power purchase agreement?
<--- Score

288. What is the best budget model for us and why?
<--- Score

289. What comes first: the project budget, or the project activities?
<--- Score

290. What are the objectives of the proposed program?
<--- Score

291. What has been accomplished so far from a communications point of view?
<--- Score

292. When are the NPV and IRR reliable?
<--- Score

293. What is ARR?
<--- Score

294. Does it serve a segment of the community not currently served?
<--- Score

295. Relevant -Do clients think the target is most important?
<--- Score

296. How can you become the company that would put you out of business?
<--- Score

297. Are you changing as fast as the world around you?
<--- Score

298. What projects are going on in the organization today, and what resources are those projects using

from the resource pools?
<--- Score

299. What are the barriers to increased Power purchase agreement production?
<--- Score

300. What is the difference between mandatory and discretionary capital investments?
<--- Score

301. How do you engage the workforce, in addition to satisfying them?
<--- Score

302. Do you have the right people on the bus?
<--- Score

303. What are our unit' s strengths and weaknesses?
<--- Score

304. How do you maintain Power purchase agreement's Integrity?
<--- Score

305. What is it like to work for you?
<--- Score

306. What threat is Power purchase agreement addressing?
<--- Score

307. How do you track customer value, profitability or financial return, organizational success, and sustainability?

<--- Score

308. Are you making progress, and are you making progress as Power purchase agreement leaders?
<--- Score

309. What information is critical to your organization that your executives are ignoring?
<--- Score

310. Who are four people whose careers you have enhanced?
<--- Score

311. Within the Successful Young Producer group, do certain types of young producers validate faster than others?
<--- Score

312. What challenges have you experienced in utilizing performance-based budgeting?
<--- Score

313. What is Capital rationing?
<--- Score

314. Does training account for various working environments (home, office, contractors)?
<--- Score

315. Has implementation been effective in reaching specified objectives so far?
<--- Score

316. How do you listen to customers to obtain actionable information?

<--- Score

317. Is My Business Ready for Government Contracting?
<--- Score

318. Have employee and contractor security responsibilities been addressed?
<--- Score

319. What is NPV?
<--- Score

320. What stupid rule would you most like to kill?
<--- Score

321. How do you foster the skills, knowledge, talents, attributes, and characteristics you want to have?
<--- Score

322. Who, on the executive team or the board, has spoken to a customer recently?
<--- Score

323. Who is the main stakeholder, with ultimate responsibility for driving Power purchase agreement forward?
<--- Score

324. How do customers see us?
<--- Score

325. Increasing importance of Integrated Marketing Communications ... Why?
<--- Score

326. How do you assess the Power purchase agreement pitfalls that are inherent in implementing it?
<--- Score

327. Why will customers want to buy your organizations products/services?
<--- Score

328. What kind of crime could a potential new hire have committed that would not only not disqualify him/her from being hired by your organization, but would actually indicate that he/she might be a particularly good fit?
<--- Score

329. Is there a work around that you can use?
<--- Score

330. What have you done to protect your business from competitive encroachment?
<--- Score

331. How do customers see your organization?
<--- Score

332. If you got fired and a new hire took your place, what would she do different?
<--- Score

333. In the past year, what have you done (or could you have done) to increase the accurate perception of your company/brand as ethical and honest?
<--- Score

334. If your customer were your grandmother, would

you tell her to buy what you're selling?
<--- Score

335. How do you determine stakeholder satisfaction and dissatisfaction?
<--- Score

336. What do you do when project lives vary significantly?
<--- Score

337. Who is responsible for errors?
<--- Score

338. How do you keep the momentum going?
<--- Score

339. Is Return on Investment addressed?
<--- Score

340. What activities must my unit perform well in order to meet customer expectations?
<--- Score

341. Do Power purchase agreement rules make a reasonable demand on a users capabilities?
<--- Score

342. What provisions should be included in a collection contract for recyclable materials?
<--- Score

343. Does the organization receive the best value in services provided by this program versus other programs?
<--- Score

344. What is the difference between a current expenditure and a capital investment?
<--- Score

345. What trouble can you get into?
<--- Score

346. Can the schedule be done in the given time?
<--- Score

347. What is Shareholder Value?
<--- Score

348. Political -is anyone trying to undermine this project?
<--- Score

349. Are all key stakeholders present at all Structured Walkthroughs?
<--- Score

350. If you do not follow, then how to lead?
<--- Score

351. What is Extended Producer Responsibility (EPR)?
<--- Score

352. What happens if you do not have enough funding?
<--- Score

353. Which project do you accept on the basis of NPV?
<--- Score

354. How long will it take to change?
<--- Score

355. What is the purpose of Power purchase agreement in relation to the mission?
<--- Score

356. What relationships among Power purchase agreement trends do you perceive?
<--- Score

357. What is MTEF?
<--- Score

358. Who will provide the final approval of Power purchase agreement deliverables?
<--- Score

359. Are you Making Progress?
<--- Score

360. Is your strategy driving your strategy? Or is the way in which you allocate resources driving your strategy?
<--- Score

361. Who are the key stakeholders?
<--- Score

362. What are the usability implications of Power purchase agreement actions?
<--- Score

363. Why is the NPV considered to be theoretically superior to all other capital budgeting techniques?

<--- Score

364. So Who Pays?
<--- Score

365. Why might a firm prefer accelerated depreciation, such as MACRS tables, to straight-line depreciation?
<--- Score

366. What is your question? Why?
<--- Score

367. Who Chooses Metrics?
<--- Score

368. Why should you adopt a Power purchase agreement framework?
<--- Score

369. Budgeting approaches - all defunct ?
<--- Score

370. What Types of Producer Contributions Are Expected?
<--- Score

371. What is the difference between an Onsite Energy Generation Energy Management Services Agreement (EMSA) and Power Purchase Agreement (PPA)?
<--- Score

372. Do we have the financial resources available?
<--- Score

373. Are Subcontractors covered in the Master Service Agreement?
<--- Score

374. What should you do if you have no alternatives to agreement and the other side is big and powerful?
<--- Score

375. Who will be responsible for deciding whether Power purchase agreement goes ahead or not after the initial investigations?
<--- Score

376. Off contract?
<--- Score

377. What are the top 3 things at the forefront of your Power purchase agreement agendas for the next 3 years?
<--- Score

378. How is the money spent?
<--- Score

379. What is it that you want to change?
<--- Score

380. Are assumptions made in Power purchase agreement stated explicitly?
<--- Score

381. What will be the geographical allocation of the media budget and why?
<--- Score

382. If you're targeting an external audience - who do you want to get your message across to?
<--- Score

383. Is it accountable?
<--- Score

384. What are the gaps in your knowledge and experience?
<--- Score

385. What must you excel at?
<--- Score

386. Who will manage the integration of tools?
<--- Score

387. Relationship between revenues and the budget?
<--- Score

Add up total points for this section:
_____ = Total points for this section

Divided by: ______ (number of statements answered) = ______ Average score for this section

Transfer your score to the Power purchase agreement Index at the beginning of the Self-Assessment.

Power purchase agreement and Managing Projects, Criteria for Project Managers:

1.0 Initiating Process Group: Power purchase agreement

1. Were sponsors and decision makers available when needed outside regularly scheduled meetings?

2. How will it affect me?

3. Measurable - are the targets measurable?

4. Where must it be done?

5. Does it make any difference if you am successful?

6. What is the NEXT thing to do?

7. What are the tools and techniques to be used in each phase?

8. How well did you do?

9. Specific - is the objective clear in terms of what, how, when, and where the situation will be changed?

10. Which of six sigmas dmaic phases focuses on the measurement of internal process that affect factors that are critical to quality?

11. Information sharing?

12. Mitigate. what will you do to minimize the impact should the risk event occur?

13. At which stage, in a typical Power purchase agreement project do stake holders have maximum

influence?

14. Are identified risks being monitored properly, are new risks arising during the Power purchase agreement project or are foreseen risks occurring?

15. How will you do it?

16. What are the pressing issues of the hour?

17. How well did the chosen processes fit the needs of the Power purchase agreement project?

18. Do you understand the quality and control criteria that must be achieved for successful Power purchase agreement project completion?

19. Are there resources to maintain and support the outcome of the Power purchase agreement project?

20. Establishment of pm office?

1.1 Project Charter: Power purchase agreement

21. What outcome, in measureable terms, are you hoping to accomplish?

22. Are you building in-house ?

23. Fit with other Products Compliments – Cannibalizes?

24. Success determination factors: how will the success of the Power purchase agreement project be determined from the customers perspective?

25. Why is a Power purchase agreement project Charter used?

26. What ideas do you have for initial tests of change (PDSA cycles)?

27. Why is it important?

28. What is the justification?

29. What are the deliverables?

30. Dependent Power purchase agreement projects: what Power purchase agreement projects must be underway or completed before this Power purchase agreement project can be successful?

31. Why Outsource?

32. What date will the task finish?

33. Why the improvements?

34. What are some examples of a business case?

35. How high should you set your goals?

36. Power purchase agreement project objective statement: what must the Power purchase agreement project do?

37. Customer benefits: what customer requirements does this Power purchase agreement project address?

38. Is time of the essence?

39. Major high-level milestone targets: what events measure progress?

40. When?

1.2 Stakeholder Register: Power purchase agreement

41. How big is the gap?

42. Who are the stakeholders?

43. Is your organization ready for change?

44. Who is managing stakeholder engagement?

45. How much influence do they have on the Power purchase agreement project?

46. How should employers make voices heard?

47. How will reports be created?

48. What are the major Power purchase agreement project milestones requiring communications or providing communications opportunities?

49. Who wants to talk about Security?

50. What opportunities exist to provide communications?

51. What & Why?

52. What is the power of the stakeholder?

1.3 Stakeholder Analysis Matrix: Power purchase agreement

53. Partnership opportunities/synergies?

54. What are the opportunities for communication?

55. Are you going to weigh the stakeholders?

56. Are you working on the right risks?

57. How much do resources cost?

58. Lack of competitive strength?

59. Are the required specifications for products or services changing?

60. Global influences?

61. Who is directly responsible for decisions on issues important to the Power purchase agreement project?

62. What is your Risk Management?

63. What advantages do your organizations stakeholders have?

64. Inoculations or payment to receive them?

65. Is changing technology threatening your organizations position?

66. What is in it for you?

67. Industry or lifestyle trends?

68. Continuity, supply chain robustness?

69. Which conditions out of the control of the management are crucial for the achievement of the outputs?

70. What should thwe organizations stakeholders avoid?

71. Does your organization have bad debt or cash-flow problems?

72. Disadvantages of proposition?

2.0 Planning Process Group: Power purchase agreement

73. What is involved in Power purchase agreement project scope management, and why is good Power purchase agreement project scope management so important on information technology Power purchase agreement projects?

74. Is the Power purchase agreement project making progress in helping to achieve the set results?

75. How well will the chosen processes produce the expected results?

76. To what extent have the target population and participants made the activities own, taking an active role in it?

77. What type of estimation method are you using?

78. What input will you be required to provide the Power purchase agreement project team?

79. If task x starts two days late, what is the effect on the Power purchase agreement project end date?

80. How will it affect you?

81. How are the principles of aid effectiveness (ownership, alignment, management for development results and mutual responsibility) being applied in the Power purchase agreement project?

82. Does the program have follow-up mechanisms (to verify the quality of the products, punctuality of delivery, etc.) to measure progress in the achievement of the envisaged results?

83. Is the identification of the problems, inequalities and gaps, with respective causes, clear in the Power purchase agreement project?

84. How well do the team follow the chosen processes?

85. If you are late, will anybody notice?

86. Is the Power purchase agreement project supported by national and/or local organizations?

87. Are the necessary foundations in place to ensure the sustainability of the results of the Power purchase agreement project?

88. What do they need to know about the Power purchase agreement project?

89. Why is it important to determine activity sequencing on Power purchase agreement projects?

90. Are the follow-up indicators relevant and do they meet the quality needed to measure the outputs and outcomes of the Power purchase agreement project?

2.1 Project Management Plan: Power purchase agreement

91. Are comparable cost estimates used for comparing, screening and selecting alternative plans, and has a reasonable cost estimate been developed for the recommended plan?

92. What does management expect of PMs?

93. Are there any windfall benefits that would accrue to the Power purchase agreement project sponsor or other parties?

94. What went right?

95. What are the known stakeholder requirements?

96. Will you add a schedule and diagram?

97. How well are you able to manage your risk?

98. Why do you manage integration?

99. What data/reports/tools/etc. do program managers need?

100. What if, for example, the positive direction and vision of your organization causes expected trends to change resulting in greater need than expected?

101. When is the Power purchase agreement project management plan created?

102. Development trends and opportunities. What if the positive direction and vision of your organization causes expected trends to change?

103. Does the selected plan protect privacy?

104. Are there non-structural buyout or relocation recommendations?

105. What are the constraints?

106. Are the proposed Power purchase agreement project purposes different than a previously authorized Power purchase agreement project?

107. Who manages integration?

108. How do you manage integration?

109. Do there need to be organizational changes?

2.2 Scope Management Plan: Power purchase agreement

110. Is documentation created for communication with the suppliers and Vendors?

111. Are stakeholders aware and supportive of the principles and practices of modern software estimation?

112. How do you plan to control Scope Creep?

113. How do you know how you are doing?

114. Are actuals compared against estimates to analyze and correct variances?

115. Have reserves been created to address risks?

116. Is there a formal set of procedures supporting Issues Management?

117. Is the schedule updated on a periodic basis?

118. Describe the process for accepting the Power purchase agreement project deliverables. Will the Power purchase agreement project deliverables become accepted in writing?

119. Have the key elements of a coherent Power purchase agreement project management strategy been established?

120. Why do you need to manage scope?

121. When will scope verification be performed?

122. Are action items captured and managed?

123. Has the budget been baselined?

124. What are the risks that could significantly affect the schedule of the Power purchase agreement project?

125. Which statement about customer expectations is not true?

126. Are issues raised, assessed, actioned, and resolved in a timely and efficient manner?

127. Have the procedures for identifying variances from estimates & adjusting the detailed work program been followed?

128. Are all payments made according to the contract(s)?

129. Are Power purchase agreement project leaders committed to this Power purchase agreement project full time?

2.3 Requirements Management Plan: Power purchase agreement

130. What went wrong?

131. Who came up with this requirement?

132. Who is responsible for quantifying the Power purchase agreement project requirements?

133. Who has the authority to reject Power purchase agreement project requirements?

134. Who will do the reporting and to whom will reports be delivered?

135. Have stakeholders been instructed in the Change Control process?

136. Why manage requirements?

137. What are you trying to do?

138. Who will approve the requirements (and if multiple approvers, in what order)?

139. Do you really need to write this document at all?

140. How knowledgeable is the primary Stakeholder(s) in the proposed application area?

141. Do you have price sheets and a methodology for determining the total proposal cost?

142. After the requirements are gathered and set forth on the requirements register, theyre little more than a laundry list of items. Some may be duplicates, some might conflict with others and some will be too broad or too vague to understand. Describe how the requirements will be analyzed. Who will perform the analysis?

143. Are actual resources expenditures versus planned expenditures acceptable?

144. How often will the reporting occur?

145. How will you communicate scheduled tasks to other team members?

146. Controlling Power purchase agreement project requirements involves monitoring the status of the Power purchase agreement project requirements and managing changes to the requirements. Who is responsible for monitoring and tracking the Power purchase agreement project requirements?

147. When and how will a requirements baseline be established in this Power purchase agreement project?

148. Is there formal agreement on who has authority to request a change in requirements?

2.4 Requirements Documentation: Power purchase agreement

149. Do your constraints stand?

150. What are current process problems?

151. Can the requirements be checked?

152. What kind of entity is a problem ?

153. How do you get the user to tell you what they want?

154. What is the risk associated with cost and schedule?

155. How does the proposed Power purchase agreement project contribute to the overall objectives of your organization?

156. Completeness. are all functions required by the customer included?

157. Is new technology needed?

158. Where do you define what is a customer, what are the attributes of customer?

159. Where do system and software requirements come from, what are sources?

160. What variations exist for a process?

161. How do you know when a Requirement is accurate enough?

162. How to document system requirements?

163. Is your business case still valid?

164. Who is interacting with the system?

165. Have the benefits identified with the system being identified clearly?

166. What are the acceptance criteria?

167. Does your organization restrict technical alternatives?

168. Who provides requirements?

2.5 Requirements Traceability Matrix: Power purchase agreement

169. What is the WBS?

170. Is there a requirements traceability process in place?

171. Do you have a clear understanding of all subcontracts in place?

172. How will it affect the stakeholders personally in their career?

173. Why use a WBS?

174. What percentage of Power purchase agreement projects are producing traceability matrices between requirements and other work products?

175. Describe the process for approving requirements so they can be added to the traceability matrix and Power purchase agreement project work can be performed. Will the Power purchase agreement project requirements become approved in writing?

176. How small is small enough?

177. Why do you manage scope?

178. How do you manage scope?

179. What are the chronologies, contingencies,

consequences, criteria?

180. Will you use a Requirements Traceability Matrix?

2.6 Project Scope Statement: Power purchase agreement

181. Elements of scope management that deal with concept development ?

182. Is an issue management process documented and filed?

183. Is there a Change Management Board?

184. What should you drop in order to add something new?

185. Is the plan under configuration management?

186. Has a method and process for requirement tracking been developed?

187. How will you haverify the accuracy of the work of the Power purchase agreement project, and what constitutes acceptance of the deliverables?

188. Will the qa related information be reported regularly as part of the status reporting mechanisms?

189. Will statistics related to QA be collected, trends analyzed, and problems raised as issues?

190. Power purchase agreement project lead, team lead, solution architect?

191. Has everyone approved the Power purchase

agreement projects scope statement?

192. What are the major deliverables of the Power purchase agreement project?

193. Have the reports to be produced, distributed, and filed been defined?

194. Has the format for tracking and monitoring schedules and costs been defined?

195. What is the product of this Power purchase agreement project?

196. Will the Power purchase agreement project risks be managed according to the Power purchase agreement projects risk management process?

197. Is your organization structure appropriate for the Power purchase agreement projects size and complexity?

198. Will all tasks resulting from issues be entered into the Power purchase agreement project Plan and tracked through the plan?

199. Have you been able to thoroughly document the Power purchase agreement projects assumptions and constraints?

200. Which risks does the Power purchase agreement project focus on?

2.7 Assumption and Constraint Log: Power purchase agreement

201. After observing execution of process, is it in compliance with the documented Plan?

202. What other teams / processes would be impacted by changes to the current process, and how?

203. What if failure during recovery?

204. Is the amount of effort justified by the anticipated value of forming a new process?

205. Contradictory information between document sections?

206. How relevant is this attribute to this Power purchase agreement project or audit?

207. Security analysis has access to information that is sanitized?

208. No superfluous information or marketing narrative?

209. Diagrams and tables are included to account for complex concepts and increase overall readability?

210. How can constraints be violated?

211. When can log be discarded?

212. Do you know what your customers expectations are regarding this process?

213. Is there documentation of system capability requirements, data requirements, environment requirements, security requirements, and computer and hardware requirements?

214. Is staff trained on the software technologies that are being used on the Power purchase agreement project?

215. Is there adequate stakeholder participation for the vetting of requirements definition, changes and management?

216. What to do at recovery?

217. What strengths do you have?

218. Is the definition of the Power purchase agreement project scope clear; what needs to be accomplished?

219. Are there unnecessary steps that are creating bottlenecks and/or causing people to wait?

220. Do the requirements meet the standards of correctness, completeness, consistency, accuracy, and readability?

2.8 Work Breakdown Structure: Power purchase agreement

221. Where does it take place?

222. How big is a work-package?

223. Do you need another level?

224. How much detail?

225. When do you stop?

226. How will you and your Power purchase agreement project team define the Power purchase agreement projects scope and work breakdown structure?

227. What is the probability of completing the Power purchase agreement project in less that xx days?

228. When would you develop a Work Breakdown Structure?

229. Is the work breakdown structure (wbs) defined and is the scope of the Power purchase agreement project clear with assigned deliverable owners?

230. How far down?

231. Why is it useful?

232. What is the probability that the Power purchase

agreement project duration will exceed xx weeks?

233. What has to be done?

234. Can you make it?

235. Who has to do it?

236. When does it have to be done?

237. How many levels?

238. Why would you develop a Work Breakdown Structure?

239. Is it still viable?

240. Is it a change in scope?

2.9 WBS Dictionary: Power purchase agreement

241. Does the contractors system provide unit costs, equivalent unit or lot costs in terms of labor, material, other direct, and indirect costs?

242. Are overhead cost budgets established for each organization which has authority to incur overhead costs?

243. Budgets assigned to control accounts?

244. Is all contract work included in the CWBS?

245. Does the contractors system description or procedures require that the performance measurement baseline plus management reserve equal the contract budget base?

246. Are significant decision points, constraints, and interfaces identified as key milestones?

247. Do the lines of authority for incurring indirect costs correspond to the lines of responsibility for management control of the same components of costs?

248. Is subcontracted work defined and identified to the appropriate subcontractor within the proper WBS element?

249. Contractor financial periods; for example,

annual?

250. Is cost performance measurement at the point in time most suitable for the category of material involved, and no earlier than the time of actual receipt of material?

251. Major functional areas of contract effort?

252. Does the contractors system identify work accomplishment against the schedule plan?

253. Are overhead costs budgets established on a basis consistent with anticipated direct business base?

254. Is the entire contract planned in time-phased control accounts to the extent practicable?

255. Is work progressively subdivided into detailed work packages as requirements are defined?

256. Are all affected work authorizations, budgeting, and scheduling documents amended to properly reflect the effects of authorized changes?

257. Are indirect costs charged to the appropriate indirect pools and incurring organization?

2.10 Schedule Management Plan: Power purchase agreement

258. Has a sponsor been identified?

259. Are the payment terms being followed?

260. Is there a formal process for updating the Power purchase agreement project baseline?

261. Has a provision been made to reassess Power purchase agreement project risks at various Power purchase agreement project stages?

262. Are Power purchase agreement project contact logs kept up to date?

263. Does a documented Power purchase agreement project organizational policy & plan (i.e. governance model) exist?

264. Does the Power purchase agreement project have a formal Power purchase agreement project Charter?

265. Power purchase agreement project definition & scope?

266. What happens if a warning is triggered?

267. Is the ims development and management approach described?

268. List all schedule constraints here. Must the Power purchase agreement project be complete by a specified date?

269. Can additional resources be added to subsequent tasks to reduce the durations of the already stated tasks?

270. How do you manage time?

271. Are the Power purchase agreement project team members located locally to the users/stakeholders?

272. Are there any activities or deliverables being added or gold-plated that could be dropped or scaled back without falling short of the original requirement?

273. Where is the scheduling tool and who has access to it to view it?

274. Do Power purchase agreement project managers participating in the Power purchase agreement project know the Power purchase agreement projects true status first hand?

275. Are schedule performance measures defined including pre-set triggers for specific actions?

276. Is your organization certified as a broker of the products/supplies?

277. Does the ims include all contract and/or designated management control milestones?

2.11 Activity List: Power purchase agreement

278. Where will it be performed?

279. In what sequence?

280. Who will perform the work?

281. Is infrastructure setup part of your Power purchase agreement project?

282. How will it be performed?

283. When will the work be performed?

284. How difficult will it be to do specific activities on this Power purchase agreement project?

285. What went well?

286. For other activities, how much delay can be tolerated?

287. How much slack is available in the Power purchase agreement project?

288. What will be performed?

289. What did not go as well?

290. The wbs is developed as part of a joint planning session. and how do you know that youhave done this

right?

291. Are the required resources available or need to be acquired?

292. How can the Power purchase agreement project be displayed graphically to better visualize the activities?

293. What are you counting on?

294. How should ongoing costs be monitored to try to keep the Power purchase agreement project within budget?

295. What is the total time required to complete the Power purchase agreement project if no delays occur?

296. What is the probability the Power purchase agreement project can be completed in xx weeks?

2.12 Activity Attributes: Power purchase agreement

297. Can you re-assign any activities to another resource to resolve an over-allocation?

298. What activity do you think you should spend the most time on?

299. What is missing?

300. How difficult will it be to do specific activities on this Power purchase agreement project?

301. How much activity detail is required?

302. Which method produces the more accurate cost assignment?

303. Has management defined a definite timeframe for the turnaround or Power purchase agreement project window?

304. How else could the items be grouped?

305. Can more resources be added?

306. Activity: what is In the Bag?

307. How many resources do you need to complete the work scope within a limit of X number of days?

308. What is the general pattern here?

309. Where else does it apply?

310. Is there anything planned that does not need to be here?

311. Resource is assigned to?

312. Have you identified the Activity Leveling Priority code value on each activity?

313. What is your organizations history in doing similar activities?

2.13 Milestone List: Power purchase agreement

314. Sustaining internal capabilities?

315. How difficult will it be to do specific activities on this Power purchase agreement project?

316. Can you derive how soon can the whole Power purchase agreement project finish?

317. How will you get the word out to customers?

318. Milestone pages should display the UserID of the person who added the milestone. Does a report or query exist that provides this audit information?

319. Information and research?

320. It is to be a narrative text providing the crucial aspects of your Power purchase agreement project proposal answering what, who, how, when and where?

321. What has been done so far?

322. Calculate how long can activity be delayed?

323. Marketing - reach, distribution, awareness?

324. Who will manage the Power purchase agreement project on a day-to-day basis?

325. Level of the Innovation?

326. How soon can the activity finish?

327. When will the Power purchase agreement project be complete?

328. Describe your organizations strengths and core competencies. What factors will make your organization succeed?

329. Usps (unique selling points)?

2.14 Network Diagram: Power purchase agreement

330. What activities must occur simultaneously with this activity?

331. What controls the start and finish of a job?

332. How difficult will it be to do specific activities on this Power purchase agreement project?

333. What can be done concurrently?

334. What are the Key Success Factors?

335. Review the logical flow of the network diagram. Take a look at which activities you have first and then sequence the activities. Do they make sense?

336. What must be completed before an activity can be started?

337. Will crashing x weeks return more in benefits than it costs?

338. What is the completion time?

339. What is the probability of completing the Power purchase agreement project in less that xx days?

340. Can you calculate the confidence level?

341. Where do you schedule uncertainty time?

342. What job or jobs follow it?

343. Are the gantt chart and/or network diagram updated periodically and used to assess the overall Power purchase agreement project timetable?

344. Exercise: what is the probability that the Power purchase agreement project duration will exceed xx weeks?

345. What activity must be completed immediately before this activity can start?

346. Planning: who, how long, what to do?

347. What activities must follow this activity?

348. Where do schedules come from?

349. What job or jobs could run concurrently?

2.15 Activity Resource Requirements: Power purchase agreement

350. Which logical relationship does the PDM use most often?

351. What is the Work Plan Standard?

352. Anything else?

353. When does monitoring begin?

354. Why do you do that?

355. Other support in specific areas?

356. How many signatures do you require on a check and does this match what is in your policy and procedures?

357. How do you handle petty cash?

358. Organizational Applicability?

359. Do you use tools like decomposition and rolling-wave planning to produce the activity list and other outputs?

360. What are constraints that you might find during the Human Resource Planning process?

361. Are there unresolved issues that need to be addressed?

362. Time for overtime?

2.16 Resource Breakdown Structure: Power purchase agreement

363. Who is allowed to see what data about which resources?

364. What can you do to improve productivity?

365. How should the information be delivered?

366. Who will be used as a Power purchase agreement project team member?

367. Changes based on input from stakeholders?

368. Why time management?

369. What is the difference between % Complete and % work?

370. Who needs what information?

371. Who will use the system?

372. What is the primary purpose of the human resource plan?

373. What are the requirements for resource data?

374. How difficult will it be to do specific activities on this Power purchase agreement project?

375. Goals for the Power purchase agreement project.

What is each stakeholders desired outcome for the Power purchase agreement project?

376. Why is this important?

377. The list could probably go on, but, the thing that you would most like to know is, How long & How much?

378. What is Power purchase agreement project communication management?

2.17 Activity Duration Estimates: Power purchase agreement

379. Is a work breakdown structure created to organize and to confirm the scope of each Power purchase agreement project?

380. Find an example of a contract for information technology services. Analyze the key features of the contract. What type of contract was used and why?

381. How do functionality, system outputs, performance, reliability, and maintainability requirements affect quality planning?

382. Who will be the main sponsor for it?

383. Consider the history of modern quality management. How have experts such as Deming, Juran, Crosby, and Taguchi affected the quality movement and todays use of Six Sigma?

384. How could you use each technique in your organization?

385. Is a contract change control system defined to manage changes to contract terms and conditions?

386. How difficult will it be to complete specific activities on this Power purchase agreement project?

387. Write a oneto two-page paper describing your dream team for this Power purchase agreement

project. What type of people would you want on your team?

388. What do you think about the WBSs for them?

389. What is pmp certification, and why do you think the number of people earning it has grown so much in the past ten years?

390. See what went wrong?

391. Which skills do you think are most important for an information technology Power purchase agreement project manager?

392. What do you think the real problem was in this case?

393. What time management activity should you do NEXT?

394. What are the advantages and disadvantages of PERT?

395. What are the key components of a Power purchase agreement project communications plan?

396. Are the required resources available?

397. What are the nine areas of expertise?

398. Are Power purchase agreement project activities decomposed into manageable components to ensure expected management control?

2.18 Duration Estimating Worksheet: Power purchase agreement

399. What work will be included in the Power purchase agreement project?

400. How can the Power purchase agreement project be displayed graphically to better visualize the activities?

401. When, then?

402. How should ongoing costs be monitored to try to keep the Power purchase agreement project within budget?

403. What utility impacts are there?

404. Is the Power purchase agreement project responsive to community need?

405. Why estimate time and cost?

406. What is the total time required to complete the Power purchase agreement project if no delays occur?

407. What are the critical bottleneck activities?

408. What is an Average Power purchase agreement project?

409. What is cost and Power purchase agreement project cost management?

410. Science = process: remember the scientific method?

411. Is this operation cost effective?

412. Small or large Power purchase agreement project?

413. Does the Power purchase agreement project provide innovative ways for stakeholders to overcome obstacles or deliver better outcomes?

414. What is next?

415. When do the individual activities need to start and finish?

416. What questions do you have?

2.19 Project Schedule: Power purchase agreement

417. Activity charts and bar charts are graphical representations of a Power purchase agreement project schedule ...how do they differ?

418. How can slack be negative?

419. Was the Power purchase agreement project schedule reviewed by all stakeholders and formally accepted?

420. What is the purpose of a Power purchase agreement project schedule?

421. Are there activities that came from a template or previous Power purchase agreement project that are not applicable on this phase of this Power purchase agreement project?

422. Are all remaining durations correct?

423. What is the difference?

424. Meet requirements?

425. Did the Power purchase agreement project come in under budget?

426. How can you shorten the schedule?

427. How does a Power purchase agreement project

get to be a year late ?

428. Master Power purchase agreement project schedule?

429. Is the Power purchase agreement project schedule available for all Power purchase agreement project team members to review?

430. How detailed should a Power purchase agreement project get?

431. Why do you need schedules?

432. Why do you need to manage Power purchase agreement project Risk?

2.20 Cost Management Plan: Power purchase agreement

433. Are changes in scope (deliverable commitments) agreed to by all affected groups & individuals?

434. Have external dependencies been captured in the schedule?

435. Is a pmo (Power purchase agreement project management office) in place and provide oversight to the Power purchase agreement project?

436. What is cost and Power purchase agreement project cost management?

437. Were Power purchase agreement project team members involved in the development of activity & task decomposition?

438. Milestones – what are the key dates in executing the contract plan?

439. Are the Power purchase agreement project plans updated on a frequent basis?

440. Owner, contractor, and subcontractors?

441. How relevant is this attribute to this Power purchase agreement project or audit?

442. Have all involved Power purchase agreement project stakeholders and work groups committed to

the Power purchase agreement project?

443. Is pert / critical path or equivalent methodology being used?

444. Quality assurance overheads?

445. Are multiple estimation methods being employed?

446. Were stakeholders aware and supportive of the principles and practices of modern software estimation?

447. Does the schedule include Power purchase agreement project management time and change request analysis time?

448. Does the Power purchase agreement project have a Statement of Work?

449. Are target dates established for each milestone deliverable?

450. Is there an issues management plan in place?

451. Are risk oriented checklists used during risk identification?

2.21 Activity Cost Estimates: Power purchase agreement

452. Based on your Power purchase agreement project communication management plan, what worked well?

453. When do you enter into PPM?

454. What is procurement?

455. What defines a successful Power purchase agreement project?

456. Vac -variance at completion, how much over/ under budget do you expect to be?

457. How do you do activity recasts?

458. Eac -estimate at completion, what is the total job expected to cost?

459. Is costing method consistent with study goals?

460. What is the Power purchase agreement projects sustainability strategy that will ensure Power purchase agreement project results will endure or be sustained?

461. One way to define activities is to consider how organization employees describe jobs to families and friends. You basically want to know, What do you do?

462. How do you change activities?

463. How difficult will it be to do specific tasks on the Power purchase agreement project?

464. Estimated cost?

465. Does the activity rely on a common set of tools to carry it out?

466. Scope statement only direct or indirect costs as well?

467. Does the estimator have experience?

468. Padding is bad and contingencies are good. what is the difference?

469. What were things that you did very well and want to do the same again on the next Power purchase agreement project?

470. How quickly can the task be done with the skills available?

2.22 Cost Estimating Worksheet: Power purchase agreement

471. Will the Power purchase agreement project collaborate with the local community and leverage resources?

472. What is the estimated labor cost today based upon this information?

473. Ask: are others positioned to know, are others credible, and will others cooperate?

474. Does the Power purchase agreement project provide innovative ways for stakeholders to overcome obstacles or deliver better outcomes?

475. What can be included?

476. Who is best positioned to know and assist in identifying corresponding factors?

477. What will others want?

478. Is it feasible to establish a control group arrangement?

479. Is the Power purchase agreement project responsive to community need?

480. Can a trend be established from historical performance data on the selected measure and are the criteria for using trend analysis or forecasting

methods met?

481. What info is needed?

482. Value pocket identification & quantification what are value pockets?

483. What costs are to be estimated?

484. What additional Power purchase agreement project(s) could be initiated as a result of this Power purchase agreement project?

485. What is the purpose of estimating?

486. What happens to any remaining funds not used?

487. How will the results be shared and to whom?

488. Identify the timeframe necessary to monitor progress and collect data to determine how the selected measure has changed?

2.23 Cost Baseline: Power purchase agreement

489. For what purpose ?

490. Has the Power purchase agreement projected annual cost to operate and maintain the product(s) or service(s) been approved and funded?

491. What is the most important thing to do next to make your Power purchase agreement project successful?

492. What can go wrong?

493. What is the consequence?

494. Is request in line with priorities?

495. Does the suggested change request represent a desired enhancement to the products functionality?

496. Have the resources used by the Power purchase agreement project been reassigned to other units or Power purchase agreement projects?

497. Is the requested change request a result of changes in other Power purchase agreement project(s)?

498. Definition of done can be traced back to the definitions of what are you providing to the customer in terms of deliverables?

499. Have the lessons learned been filed with the Power purchase agreement project Management Office?

500. At which frequency ?

501. Will the Power purchase agreement project fail if the change request is not executed?

502. Is the cr within Power purchase agreement project scope?

503. What weaknesses do you have?

504. On time?

505. Are there contingencies or conditions related to the acceptance?

506. How difficult will it be to do specific tasks on the Power purchase agreement project?

2.24 Quality Management Plan: Power purchase agreement

507. How do you decide who is responsible for signing the data reports?

508. Have all involved stakeholders and work groups committed to the Power purchase agreement project?

509. Who else should be involved ?

510. Were the right locations/samples tested for the right parameters?

511. Has a Power purchase agreement project Communications Plan been developed?

512. How does your organization address regulatory, legal, and ethical compliance?

513. What are the appropriate test methods to be used?

514. How do you decide what information needs to be recorded?

515. How does your organization maintain a safe and healthy work environment?

516. What changes can you make that will result in improvement?

517. Can you perform this task or activity in a more

effective manner?

518. Are you following the quality standards?

519. How do you ensure that your sampling methods and procedures meet your data quality objectives?

520. How do you field-modify testing procedures?

521. What are the established criteria that sampling / testing data are compared against?

522. How does your organization make it easy for customers to seek assistance or complain?

523. Does the Power purchase agreement project have a formal Power purchase agreement project Plan?

524. How are senior leaders, employees, and your organization involved in supporting the community?

525. How do you measure?

526. How does your organization ensure the reliability, accuracy, timeliness, security and accessibility of data and information?

2.25 Quality Metrics: Power purchase agreement

527. What are you trying to accomplish?

528. Which data do others need in one place to target areas of improvement?

529. Are documents on hand to provide explanations of privacy and confidentiality?

530. How do you communicate results and findings to upper management?

531. How do you know if everyone is trying to improve the right things?

532. Has it met internal or external standards?

533. Was the overall quality better or worse than previous products?

534. Was material distributed on time?

535. Are interface issues coordinated?

536. What is the timeline to meet your goal?

537. Has trace of defects been initiated?

538. Is there alignment within your organization on definitions?

539. Is quality culture a competitive advantage?

540. What are your organizations expectations for its quality Power purchase agreement project?

541. What documentation is required?

542. What group is empowered to define quality requirements?

543. Is a risk containment plan in place?

544. What makes a visualization memorable?

545. How should customers provide input?

546. What happens if you get an abnormal result?

2.26 Process Improvement Plan: Power purchase agreement

547. What actions are needed to address the problems and achieve the goals?

548. Have storage and access mechanisms and procedures been determined?

549. Are you meeting the quality standards?

550. To elicit goal statements, do you ask a question such as, What do you want to achieve?

551. Has a process guide to collect the data been developed?

552. Everyone agrees on what process improvement is, right?

553. Are you making progress on the goals?

554. Does explicit definition of the measures exist?

555. Have the supporting tools been developed or acquired?

556. Why do you want to achieve the goal?

557. Management commitment at all levels?

558. What is quality and how will you ensure it?

559. What is the return on investment?

560. What personnel are the coaches for your initiative?

561. Does your process ensure quality?

562. If a process improvement framework is being used, which elements will help the problems and goals listed?

563. Where do you want to be?

564. Has the time line required to move measurement results from the points of collection to databases or users been established?

2.27 Responsibility Assignment Matrix: Power purchase agreement

565. What simple tool can you use to help identify and prioritize Power purchase agreement project risks that is very low tech and high touch?

566. What travel needed?

567. What is the business need?

568. Does each activity-deliverable have exactly one Accountable responsibility, so that accountability is clear and decisions can be made quickly?

569. Are people afraid to let you know when others are under allocated?

570. Who is going to do that work?

571. Identify and isolate causes of favorable and unfavorable cost and schedule variances?

572. Budgeted cost for work performed?

573. How cost benefit analysis?

574. Incurrence of actual indirect costs in excess of budgets, by element of expense?

575. Is work properly classified as measured effort, LOE, or apportioned effort and appropriately separated?

576. Contemplated overhead expenditure for each period based on the best information currently available?

577. Are data elements reconcilable between internal summary reports and reports forwarded to stakeholders?

578. Is it safe to say you can handle more work or that some tasks you are supposed to do arent worth doing?

579. Undistributed budgets, if any?

580. Does each role with Accountable responsibility have the authority within your organization to make the required decisions?

581. Will too many Signing-off responsibilities delay the completion of the activity/deliverable?

582. Evaluate the performance of operating organizations?

2.28 Roles and Responsibilities: Power purchase agreement

583. What should you do now to ensure that you are meeting all expectations of your current position?

584. How well did the Power purchase agreement project Team understand the expectations of specific roles and responsibilities?

585. Was the expectation clearly communicated?

586. Is the data complete?

587. What should you highlight for improvement?

588. Required skills, knowledge, experience?

589. Does the team have access to and ability to use data analysis tools?

590. Implementation of actions: Who are the responsible units?

591. Who is responsible for implementation activities and where will the functions, roles and responsibilities be defined?

592. What should you do now to prepare yourself for a promotion, increased responsibilities or a different job?

593. Is there a training program in place for

stakeholders covering expectations, roles and responsibilities and any addition knowledge others need to be good stakeholders?

594. Do you take the time to clearly define roles and responsibilities on Power purchase agreement project tasks?

595. Do the values and practices inherent in the culture of your organization foster or hinder the process?

596. What should you do now to ensure that you are exceeding expectations and excelling in your current position?

597. Once the responsibilities are defined for the Power purchase agreement project, have the deliverables, roles and responsibilities been clearly communicated to every participant?

598. Who is involved?

599. Who is responsible for each task?

600. What areas would you highlight for changes or improvements?

601. Does your vision/mission support a culture of quality data?

602. Concern: where are you limited or have no authority, where you can not influence?

2.29 Human Resource Management Plan: Power purchase agreement

603. Have stakeholder accountabilities & responsibilities been clearly defined?

604. Is the communication plan being followed?

605. Were escalated issues resolved promptly?

606. Are quality metrics defined?

607. Personnel with expertise?

608. Do all stakeholders know how to access this repository and where to find the Power purchase agreement project documentation?

609. Are adequate resources provided for the quality assurance function?

610. What areas does the group agree are the biggest success on the Power purchase agreement project?

611. Was the Power purchase agreement project schedule reviewed by all stakeholders and formally accepted?

612. Is the Power purchase agreement project sponsor clearly communicating the business case or rationale for why this Power purchase agreement project is needed?

613. Have all necessary approvals been obtained?

614. Have process improvement efforts been completed before requirements efforts begin?

615. Is a stakeholder management plan in place that covers topics?

616. Is there a formal set of procedures supporting Stakeholder Management?

617. Were stakeholders aware and supportive of the principles and practices of modern cost estimation?

618. Power purchase agreement project Objectives?

619. Are change requests logged and managed?

620. Has your organization readiness assessment been conducted?

2.30 Communications Management Plan: Power purchase agreement

621. Can you think of other people who might have concerns or interests?

622. What communications method?

623. How often do you engage with stakeholders?

624. What are the interrelationships?

625. Why manage stakeholders?

626. Is there an important stakeholder who is actively opposed and will not receive messages?

627. What is the stakeholders level of authority?

628. Do you feel a register helps?

629. How were corresponding initiatives successful?

630. What to know?

631. What data is going to be required?

632. What approaches do you use?

633. Who is responsible?

634. Are there potential barriers between the team and the stakeholder?

635. How do you manage communications?

636. How did the term stakeholder originate?

637. Are you constantly rushing from meeting to meeting?

638. Conflict resolution -which method when?

639. In your work, how much time is spent on stakeholder identification?

640. Who is involved as you identify stakeholders?

2.31 Risk Management Plan: Power purchase agreement

641. What risks are tracked?

642. Market risk: will the new product be useful to your organization or marketable to others?

643. Degree of confidence in estimated size estimate?

644. How is the audit profession changing?

645. Are there new risks that mitigation strategies might introduce?

646. Are there risks to human health or the environment that need to be controlled or mitigated?

647. What are the chances the risk event will occur?

648. Why might it be late?

649. Are status updates being made on schedule and are the updates clearly described?

650. What is the impact to the Power purchase agreement project if the item is not resolved in a timely fashion?

651. If you can not fix it, how do you do it differently?

652. Where are you confronted with risks during the business phases?

653. How much risk can you tolerate?

654. Premium on reliability of product?

655. How quickly does this item need to be resolved?

656. Is the process supported by tools?

657. What will drive change?

658. How is implementation of risk actions performed?

659. What are some questions that should be addressed in a risk management plan?

660. Does the software engineering team have the right mix of skills?

2.32 Risk Register: Power purchase agreement

661. User involvement: do you have the right users?

662. What should you do now?

663. Why would you develop a risk register?

664. Contingency actions - planned actions to reduce the immediate seriousness of the risk when it does occur. What should you do when?

665. Assume the risk event or situation happens, what would the impact be?

666. What are your key risks/show istoppers and what is being done to manage them?

667. Financial risk -can your organization afford to undertake the Power purchase agreement project?

668. Who is going to do it?

669. What is the reason for current performance gaps and do the risks and opportunities identified previously account for this?

670. What may happen or not go according to plan?

671. Is further information required before making a decision?

672. Manageability – have mitigations to the risk been identified?

673. Can the likelihood and impact of failing to achieve corresponding recommendations and action plans be assessed?

674. What is your current and future risk profile?

675. What is the probability and impact of the risk occurring?

676. Technology risk -is the Power purchase agreement project technically feasible?

677. Risk probability and impact: how will the probabilities and impacts of risk items be assessed?

678. Are there other alternative controls that could be implemented?

679. Assume the event happens, what is the Most Likely impact?

2.33 Probability and Impact Assessment: Power purchase agreement

680. Does the Power purchase agreement project team have experience with the technology to be implemented?

681. Have customers been involved fully in the definition of requirements?

682. What risks are necessary to achieve success?

683. Monitoring of the overall Power purchase agreement project status – are there any changes in the Power purchase agreement project that can effect and cause new possible risks?

684. Do you have a mechanism for managing change?

685. Are Power purchase agreement project requirements stable?

686. What are the levels of understanding of the future users of the outcome/results of this Power purchase agreement project?

687. Who should be notified of the occurrence of each of the risk indicators?

688. Are tools for analysis and design available?

689. Do end-users have realistic expectations?

690. How do the products attain the specifications?

691. What is the level of experience available with your organization?

692. What are the current or emerging trends of culture?

693. Has the need for the Power purchase agreement project been properly established?

694. How will the consumption pattern change?

695. Are testing tools available and suitable?

696. Have decisions that should be left open because of inadequate information on technology been identified and responsibility assigned for reducing the uncertainty?

697. Will there be an increase in the political conservatism?

698. What are the risks involved in appointing external agencies to manage the Power purchase agreement project?

699. What is the probability of the risk occurring?

2.34 Probability and Impact Matrix: Power purchase agreement

700. Which is the BEST thing to do?

701. What is the likelihood of a breakthrough?

702. Are the risk data complete?

703. Have you ascribed a level of confidence to every critical technical objective?

704. How is the risk management process used in practice?

705. Do you need a risk management plan?

706. Are Power purchase agreement project requirements stable?

707. What are the methods to deal with risks?

708. Is a software Power purchase agreement project management tool available?

709. How would you suggest monitoring for risk transition indicators?

710. What kind of preparation would be required to do this?

711. What should be the level of difficulty in handling the technology?

712. Has something like this been done before?

713. While preparing your risk responses, you identify additional risks. What should you do?

714. How are risks and risk management perceived in the Power purchase agreement project?

715. What should you do FIRST?

2.35 Risk Data Sheet: Power purchase agreement

716. How can it happen?

717. Has the most cost-effective solution been chosen?

718. Risk of what?

719. What are you weak at and therefore need to do better?

720. How do you handle product safely?

721. What can happen?

722. How reliable is the data source?

723. What are the main threats to your existence?

724. Will revised controls lead to tolerable risk levels?

725. What if client refuses?

726. Has a sensitivity analysis been carried out?

727. Potential for recurrence?

728. What do you know?

729. What actions can be taken to eliminate or remove risk?

730. What can you do?

731. What is the duration of infection (the length of time the host is infected with the organizm) in a normal healthy human host?

732. Type of risk identified?

733. If it happens, what are the consequences?

734. What are you trying to achieve (Objectives)?

735. Do effective diagnostic tests exist?

2.36 Procurement Management Plan: Power purchase agreement

736. Are risk triggers captured?

737. Are the schedule estimates reasonable given the Power purchase agreement project?

738. Is quality monitored from the perspective of the customers needs and expectations?

739. Financial capacity; does the seller have, or can the seller reasonably be expected to obtain, the financial resources needed?

740. Is the structure for tracking the Power purchase agreement project schedule well defined and assigned to a specific individual?

741. Has the business need been clearly defined?

742. Have the key functions and capabilities been defined and assigned to each release or iteration?

743. Are the quality tools and methods identified in the Quality Plan appropriate to the Power purchase agreement project?

744. Has the scope management document been updated and distributed to help prevent scope creep?

745. Are the appropriate IT resources adequate to meet planned commitments?

746. Has a quality assurance plan been developed for the Power purchase agreement project?

747. Are status reports received per the Power purchase agreement project Plan?

748. Is there a procurement management plan in place?

749. Are enough systems & user personnel assigned to the Power purchase agreement project?

750. Does the schedule include Power purchase agreement project management time and change request analysis time?

751. What were things that you did very well and want to do the same again on the next Power purchase agreement project?

2.37 Source Selection Criteria: Power purchase agreement

752. In order of importance, which evaluation criteria are the most critical to the determination of your overall rating?

753. Are types/quantities of material, facilities appropriate?

754. If the costs are normalized, please account for how the normalization is conducted. Is a cost realism analysis used?

755. How much past performance information should be requested?

756. Can you reasonably estimate total organization requirements for the coming year?

757. What instructions should be provided regarding oral presentations?

758. What source selection software is your team using?

759. Can you identify proposed teaming partners and/or subcontractors and consider the nature and extent of proposed involvement in satisfying the Power purchase agreement project requirements?

760. How are clarifications and communications appropriately used?

761. What is the role of counsel in the procurement process?

762. How important is cost in the source selection decision relative to past performance and technical considerations?

763. How do you consolidate reviews and analysis of evaluators?

764. How long will it take for the purchase cost to be the same as the lease cost?

765. What common questions or problems are associated with debriefings?

766. How do you encourage efficiency and consistency?

767. What are the guidelines regarding award without considerations?

768. In which phase of the acquisition process cycle does source qualifications reside?

769. What should a Draft Request for Proposal (DRFP) include?

770. What evidence should be provided regarding proposal evaluations?

771. How will you evaluate offerors proposals?

2.38 Stakeholder Management Plan: Power purchase agreement

772. Are the people assigned to the Power purchase agreement project sufficiently qualified?

773. Has the schedule been baselined?

774. Can the requirements be traced to the appropriate components of the solution, as well as test scripts?

775. Are the quality tools and methods identified in the Quality Plan appropriate to the Power purchase agreement project?

776. Have all team members been part of identifying risks?

777. Is stakeholder involvement adequate?

778. Are assumptions being identified, recorded, analyzed, qualified and closed?

779. Does the role of the Power purchase agreement project Team cease upon the delivery of the Power purchase agreement projects outputs?

780. Has a provision been made to reassess Power purchase agreement project risks at various Power purchase agreement project stages?

781. Is it standard practice to formally commit

stakeholders to the Power purchase agreement project via agreements?

782. What are the criteria for selecting other suppliers, including subcontractors?

783. What training requirements are there based upon the required skills and resources?

784. At what point will the Power purchase agreement project be closed and what will be done to formally close the Power purchase agreement project?

785. Is there an onboarding process in place?

786. Does the business case include how the Power purchase agreement project aligns with your organizations strategic goals & objectives?

787. Why would a customer be interested in a particular product or service?

2.39 Change Management Plan: Power purchase agreement

788. Does this change represent a completely new process for your organization, or a different application of an existing process?

789. What does a resilient organization look like?

790. What risks may occur upfront, during implementation and after implementation?

791. Where will the funds come from?

792. Different application of an existing process?

793. What is the reason for the communication?

794. Is a training information sheet available?

795. Has the target training audience been identified and nominated?

796. Identify the risk and assess the significance and likelihood of it occurring and plan the contingency What risks may occur upfront?

797. Are there any restrictions on who can receive the communications?

798. What method and medium would you use to announce a message?

799. What time commitment will this involve?

800. Impact of systems implementation on organization change?

801. How many people are required in each of the roles?

802. Would you need to tailor a special message for each segment of the audience?

803. What goal(s) do you hope to accomplish?

804. What new competencies will be required for the roles?

805. Which relationships will change?

806. How will the stakeholders share information and transfer knowledge?

3.0 Executing Process Group: Power purchase agreement

807. What business situation is being addressed?

808. Based on your Power purchase agreement project communication management plan, what worked well?

809. What is involved in the solicitation process?

810. Have operating capacities been created and/or reinforced in partners?

811. Would you rate yourself as being risk-averse, risk-neutral, or risk-seeking?

812. What does it mean to take a systems view of a Power purchase agreement project?

813. What are the main types of goods and services being outsourced?

814. Is activity definition the first process involved in Power purchase agreement project time management?

815. After how many days will the lease cost be the same as the purchase cost for the equipment?

816. What will you do to minimize the impact should a risk event occur?

817. On which process should team members spend the most time?

818. What good practices or successful experiences or transferable examples have been identified?

819. How well did the team follow the chosen processes?

820. Do Power purchase agreement project managers understand your organizational context for Power purchase agreement projects?

821. What are the challenges Power purchase agreement project teams face?

822. How does Power purchase agreement project management relate to other disciplines?

823. How will professionals learn what is expected from them what the deliverables are?

824. Who are the Power purchase agreement project stakeholders?

825. Are escalated issues resolved promptly?

826. What are deliverables of your Power purchase agreement project?

3.1 Team Member Status Report: Power purchase agreement

827. How it is to be done?

828. How can you make it practical?

829. Are the attitudes of staff regarding Power purchase agreement project work improving?

830. How does this product, good, or service meet the needs of the Power purchase agreement project and your organization as a whole?

831. The problem with Reward & Recognition Programs is that the truly deserving people all too often get left out. How can you make it practical?

832. When a teams productivity and success depend on collaboration and the efficient flow of information, what generally fails them?

833. Does every department have to have a Power purchase agreement project Manager on staff?

834. Are the products of your organizations Power purchase agreement projects meeting customers objectives?

835. What specific interest groups do you have in place?

836. How will resource planning be done?

837. Do you have an Enterprise Power purchase agreement project Management Office (EPMO)?

838. Will the staff do training or is that done by a third party?

839. What is to be done?

840. Are your organizations Power purchase agreement projects more successful over time?

841. Is there evidence that staff is taking a more professional approach toward management of your organizations Power purchase agreement projects?

842. How much risk is involved?

843. Why is it to be done?

844. Does the product, good, or service already exist within your organization?

845. Does your organization have the means (staff, money, contract, etc.) to produce or to acquire the product, good, or service?

3.2 Change Request: Power purchase agreement

846. How does a team identify the discrete elements of a configuration?

847. Are you implementing itil processes?

848. Who has responsibility for approving and ranking changes?

849. How is quality being addressed on the Power purchase agreement project?

850. How many lines of code must be changed to implement the change?

851. What are the requirements for urgent changes?

852. How does your organization control changes before and after software is released to a customer?

853. What should be regulated in a change control operating instruction?

854. Change request coordination ?

855. How are the measures for carrying out the change established?

856. How shall the implementation of changes be recorded?

857. What must be taken into consideration when introducing change control programs?

858. What has an inspector to inspect and to check?

859. What type of changes does change control take into account?

860. Who is responsible to authorize changes?

861. What is the relationship between requirements attributes and attributes like complexity and size?

862. Will all change requests and current status be logged?

863. Why do you want to have a change control system?

864. What is a Change Request Form?

865. Will new change requests be acknowledged in a timely manner?

3.3 Change Log: Power purchase agreement

866. Is the change request open, closed or pending?

867. Should a more thorough impact analysis be conducted?

868. Is this a mandatory replacement?

869. How does this change affect the timeline of the schedule?

870. Is the change request within Power purchase agreement project scope?

871. Is the submitted change a new change or a modification of a previously approved change?

872. Where do changes come from?

873. Will the Power purchase agreement project fail if the change request is not executed?

874. Does the suggested change request seem to represent a necessary enhancement to the product?

875. Do the described changes impact on the integrity or security of the system?

876. When was the request submitted?

877. When was the request approved?

878. Who initiated the change request?

879. How does this relate to the standards developed for specific business processes?

880. Is the requested change request a result of changes in other Power purchase agreement project(s)?

881. Is the change backward compatible without limitations?

882. How does this change affect scope?

3.4 Decision Log: Power purchase agreement

883. What was the rationale for the decision?

884. What eDiscovery problem or issue did your organization set out to fix or make better?

885. What makes you different or better than others companies selling the same thing?

886. How do you know when you are achieving it?

887. What are the cost implications?

888. Does anything need to be adjusted?

889. Who is the decisionmaker?

890. Do strategies and tactics aimed at less than full control reduce the costs of management or simply shift the cost burden?

891. How does an increasing emphasis on cost containment influence the strategies and tactics used?

892. Decision-making process; how will the team make decisions?

893. How does provision of information, both in terms of content and presentation, influence acceptance of alternative strategies?

894. Behaviors; what are guidelines that the team has identified that will assist them with getting the most out of team meetings?

895. Which variables make a critical difference?

896. What alternatives/risks were considered?

897. Who will be given a copy of this document and where will it be kept?

898. Adversarial environment. is your opponent open to a non-traditional workflow, or will it likely challenge anything you do?

899. It becomes critical to track and periodically revisit both operational effectiveness; Are you noticing all that you need to, and are you interpreting what you see effectively?

900. Linked to original objective?

901. Meeting purpose; why does this team meet?

902. How effective is maintaining the log at facilitating organizational learning?

3.5 Quality Audit: Power purchase agreement

903. Is refuse and garbage adequately stored and disposed of with sufficient frequency to prevent contamination?

904. How does your organization know that the range and quality of its social and recreational services and facilities are appropriately effective and constructive in meeting the needs of staff?

905. What is the collective experience of the team to be assigned to an audit?

906. How does your organization know that its relationship with its (past) staff is appropriately effective and constructive?

907. How does your organization know that its staff embody the core knowledge, skills and characteristics for which it wishes to be recognized?

908. How does your organization know that its planning processes are appropriately effective and constructive?

909. How do you know what, specifically, is required of you in your work?

910. How does your organization know that its staff have appropriate access to a fair and effective grievance process?

911. How does your organization know that its system for managing intellectual property issues is appropriately effective, constructive and fair?

912. How does your organization know that it provides a safe and healthy environment?

913. How do staff know if they are doing a good job?

914. Are all areas associated with the storage and reconditioning of devices clean, free of rubbish, adequately ventilated and in good repair?

915. How does your organization know that its relationships with relevant professional bodies are appropriately effective and constructive?

916. What will the Observer get to Observe?

917. Does the audit organization have experience in performing the required work for entities of your type and size?

918. Are the policies and processes, as set out in the Quality Audit Manual, properly applied?

919. Do the suppliers use a formal quality system?

920. How does your organization know that the range and quality of its accommodation, catering and transportation services are appropriately effective and constructive?

921. What does an analysis of your organizations staff profile suggest in terms of its planning, and how is

this being addressed?

922. Is there any content that may be legally actionable?

3.6 Team Directory: Power purchase agreement

923. Process decisions: are contractors adequately prosecuting the work?

924. Who are the Team Members?

925. How and in what format should information be presented?

926. Where will the product be used and/or delivered or built when appropriate?

927. Who will report Power purchase agreement project status to all stakeholders?

928. Who will talk to the customer?

929. Where should the information be distributed?

930. Process decisions: how well was task order work performed?

931. Who are your stakeholders (customers, sponsors, end users, team members)?

932. How do unidentified risks impact the outcome of the Power purchase agreement project?

933. Process decisions: which organizational elements and which individuals will be assigned management functions?

934. Have you decided when to celebrate the Power purchase agreement projects completion date?

935. How will you accomplish and manage the objectives?

936. Process decisions: are there any statutory or regulatory issues relevant to the timely execution of work?

937. Contract requirements complied with?

938. Process decisions: are all start-up, turn over and close out requirements of the contract satisfied?

939. Decisions: is the most suitable form of contract being used?

940. Timing: when do the effects of communication take place?

941. Process decisions: is work progressing on schedule and per contract requirements?

942. How will the team handle changes?

3.7 Team Operating Agreement: Power purchase agreement

943. What is the anticipated procedure (recruitment, solicitation of volunteers, or assignment) for selecting team members?

944. Do you leverage technology engagement tools group chat, polls, screen sharing, etc.?

945. To whom do you deliver your services?

946. Are leadership responsibilities shared among team members (versus a single leader)?

947. Confidentiality: how will confidential information be handled?

948. What is a Virtual Team?

949. Must your members collaborate successfully to complete Power purchase agreement projects?

950. How does teaming fit in with overall organizational goals and meet organizational needs?

951. Did you recap the meeting purpose, time, and expectations?

952. How will you divide work equitably?

953. How will your group handle planned absences?

954. What types of accommodations will be formulated and put in place for sustaining the team?

955. What are the current caseload numbers in the unit?

956. Communication protocols: how will the team communicate?

957. Does your team need access to all documents and information at all times?

958. Do you ask participants to close laptops and place mobile devices on silent on the table while the meeting is in progress?

959. Do you vary your voice pace, tone and pitch to engage participants and gain involvement?

960. Have you established procedures that team members can follow to work effectively together, such as a team operating agreement?

961. Did you prepare participants for the next meeting?

962. Do you use a parking lot for any items that are important and outside of the agenda?

3.8 Team Performance Assessment: Power purchase agreement

963. To what degree are the relative importance and priority of the goals clear to all team members?

964. To what degree will team members, individually and collectively, commit time to help themselves and others learn and develop skills?

965. Delaying market entry: how long is too long?

966. When does the medium matter?

967. How do you encourage members to learn from each other?

968. Is there a particular method of data analysis that you would recommend as a means of demonstrating that method variance is not of great concern for a given dataset?

969. To what degree are the goals ambitious?

970. To what degree does the teams purpose contain themes that are particularly meaningful and memorable?

971. To what degree will new and supplemental skills be introduced as the need is recognized?

972. How much interpersonal friction is there in your team?

973. To what degree do the goals specify concrete team work products?

974. To what degree are the goals realistic?

975. To what degree are the skill areas critical to team performance present?

976. Do friends perform better than acquaintances?

977. To what degree can team members frequently and easily communicate with one another?

978. To what degree do members understand and articulate the same purpose without relying on ambiguous abstractions?

979. What are teams?

980. To what degree do team members agree with the goals, relative importance, and the ways in which achievement will be measured?

981. What do you think is the most constructive thing that could be done now to resolve considerations and disputes about method variance?

982. Where to from here?

3.9 Team Member Performance Assessment: Power purchase agreement

983. How do you implement Cost Reduction?

984. Does statute or regulation require the job responsibility?

985. To what degree does the teams approach to its work allow for modification and improvement over time?

986. What are acceptable governance changes?

987. What are the key duties or tasks of the Ratee?

988. What, if any, steps are available for employees who feel they have been unfairly or inaccurately rated?

989. Does platform-specific assessment information contribute to training placement or tailoring of instruction (e.g. aptitude-treatment interaction)?

990. Verify business objectives. Are they appropriate, and well-articulated?

991. What steps have you taken to improve performance?

992. What is collaboration?

993. Is it clear how goals will be accomplished?

994. What is the role of the Reviewer?

995. What evaluation results do you have?

996. Are any governance changes sufficient to impact achievement?

997. What were the challenges that resulted for training and assessment?

998. What instructional strategies were developed/ incorporated (e.g., direct instruction, indirect instruction, experiential learning, independent study, interactive instruction)?

999. Can your organization rate by exception and assume that most employees are performing at an acceptable level?

1000. Should a ratee get a copy of all the raters documents about the employees performance?

1001. What are the evaluation strategies (e.g., reaction, learning, behavior, results) used. What evaluation results did you have?

3.10 Issue Log: Power purchase agreement

1002. Is access to the Issue Log controlled?

1003. Do you have members of your team responsible for certain stakeholders?

1004. Are the stakeholders getting the information they need, are they consulted, are concerns addressed?

1005. Who reported the issue?

1006. Are the Power purchase agreement project issues uniquely identified, including to which product they refer?

1007. What help do you and your team need from the stakeholders?

1008. How do you reply to this question; you am new here and managing this major program. How do you suggest you build your network?

1009. What approaches to you feel are the best ones to use?

1010. What would have to change?

1011. Why not more evaluators?

1012. Are stakeholder roles recognized by your

organization?

1013. Do you often overlook a key stakeholder or stakeholder group?

1014. Can an impact cause deviation beyond team, stage or Power purchase agreement project tolerances?

1015. What steps can you take for positive relationships?

1016. Are they needed?

1017. Which stakeholders can influence others?

1018. Who are the members of the governing body?

1019. Why multiple evaluators?

4.0 Monitoring and Controlling Process Group: Power purchase agreement

1020. What were things that you did well, and could improve, and how?

1021. How was the program set-up initiated?

1022. Is there adequate validation on required fields?

1023. Did the Power purchase agreement project team have enough people to execute the Power purchase agreement project plan?

1024. Is the schedule for the set products being met?

1025. What is the timeline for the Power purchase agreement project?

1026. How were collaborations developed, and how are they sustained?

1027. What are the goals of the program?

1028. Do the products created live up to the necessary quality?

1029. What resources are necessary?

1030. Is there sufficient time allotted between the general system design and the detailed system design phases?

1031. What were things that you need to improve?

1032. How is agile portfolio management done?

1033. Were decisions made in a timely manner?

1034. What input will you be required to provide the Power purchase agreement project team?

1035. Do the partners have sufficient financial capacity to keep up the benefits produced by the programme?

1036. Contingency planning. if a risk event occurs, what will you do?

1037. How is agile program management done?

1038. Use: how will they use the information?

4.1 Project Performance Report: Power purchase agreement

1039. To what degree can all members engage in open and interactive considerations?

1040. To what degree does the funding match the requirement?

1041. To what degree is there a sense that only the team can succeed?

1042. To what degree are the demands of the task compatible with and converge with the relationships of the informal organization?

1043. To what degree are the tasks requirements reflected in the flow and storage of information?

1044. To what degree do team members articulate the teams work approach?

1045. To what degree do all members feel responsible for all agreed-upon measures?

1046. To what degree is the team cognizant of small wins to be celebrated along the way?

1047. To what degree will each member have the opportunity to advance his or her professional skills in all three of the above categories while contributing to the accomplishment of the teams purpose and goals?

1048. To what degree does the formal organization make use of individual resources and meet individual needs?

1049. To what degree are the members clear on what they are individually responsible for and what they are jointly responsible for?

1050. To what degree are the teams goals and objectives clear, simple, and measurable?

1051. To what degree are the demands of the task compatible with and converge with the mission and functions of the formal organization?

1052. To what degree can the team measure progress against specific goals?

1053. To what degree can team members vigorously define the teams purpose in considerations with others who are not part of the functioning team?

1054. To what degree can team members meet frequently enough to accomplish the teams ends?

4.2 Variance Analysis: Power purchase agreement

1055. Are indirect costs accumulated for comparison with the corresponding budgets?

1056. How are material, labor, and overhead variances calculated and recorded?

1057. Are there changes in the overhead pool and/or organization structures?

1058. The anticipated business volume?

1059. Are your organizations and items of cost assigned to each pool identified?

1060. What types of services and expense are shared between business segments?

1061. Are there knowledgeable Power purchase agreement projections of future performance?

1062. What does a favorable labor efficiency variance mean?

1063. Are authorized changes being incorporated in a timely manner?

1064. What is the expected future profitability of each customer?

1065. Did your organization lose existing customers

and/or gain new customers?

1066. Are the actual costs used for variance analysis reconcilable with data from the accounting system?

1067. Are all authorized tasks assigned to identified organizational elements?

1068. Do work packages consist of discrete tasks which are adequately described?

1069. Are the bases and rates for allocating costs from each indirect pool consistently applied?

1070. There are detailed schedules which support control account and work package start and completion dates/events?

1071. Who are responsible for the establishment of budgets and assignment of resources for overhead performance?

1072. Favorable or unfavorable variance?

4.3 Earned Value Status: Power purchase agreement

1073. Are you hitting your Power purchase agreement projects targets?

1074. How much is it going to cost by the finish?

1075. Where are your problem areas?

1076. Verification is a process of ensuring that the developed system satisfies the stakeholders agreements and specifications; Are you building the product right? What do you haverify?

1077. What is the unit of forecast value?

1078. Where is evidence-based earned value in your organization reported?

1079. When is it going to finish?

1080. How does this compare with other Power purchase agreement projects?

1081. Earned value can be used in almost any Power purchase agreement project situation and in almost any Power purchase agreement project environment. it may be used on large Power purchase agreement projects, medium sized Power purchase agreement projects, tiny Power purchase agreement projects (in cut-down form), complex and simple Power purchase agreement projects and in any market sector. some people, of course, know all about earned value, they have used it for years - but perhaps not as effectively as they could have?

1082. If earned value management (EVM) is so good in determining the true status of a Power purchase agreement project and Power purchase agreement project its completion, why is it that hardly any one uses it in information systems related Power purchase agreement projects?

1083. Validation is a process of ensuring that the developed system will actually achieve the stakeholders desired outcomes; Are you building the right product? What do you validate?

4.4 Risk Audit: Power purchase agreement

1084. Has everyone (staff, volunteers and participants) agreed to a code of behaviour or conduct?

1085. Have you considered the health and safety of everyone in your organization and do you meet work health and safety regulations?

1086. How effective are your risk controls?

1087. Are all programs planned and conducted according to recognized safety standards?

1088. Mitigation -how can you avoid the risk?

1089. Which assets are important?

1090. Do you have a clear plan for the future that describes what you want to do and how you are going to do it?

1091. Who is responsible for what?

1092. Is the auditor able to evaluate contradictory evidence in an unbiased manner?

1093. Are auditors able to effectively apply more soft evidence found in the risk-assessment process with the results of more tangible audit evidence found through more substantive testing?

1094. Will an appropriate standard of care be applied to all involved?

1095. Are requirements fully understood by the team and customers?

1096. Are tool mentors available?

1097. Are audit program plans risk-adjusted?

1098. Is your organization willing to commit significant time to the requirements gathering process?

1099. Are corresponding safety and risk management policies posted for all to see?

1100. How are risk appetites expressed?

1101. Are team members trained in the use of the tools?

1102. Strategic business risk audit methodologies; are corresponding an attempt to sell other services, and is management becoming the client of the audit rather than the shareholder?

1103. Does willful intent modify risk-based auditing?

4.5 Contractor Status Report: Power purchase agreement

1104. Describe how often regular updates are made to the proposed solution. Are corresponding regular updates included in the standard maintenance plan?

1105. Are there contractual transfer concerns?

1106. What was the budget or estimated cost for your organizations services?

1107. How long have you been using the services?

1108. What was the overall budget or estimated cost?

1109. How does the proposed individual meet each requirement?

1110. What was the final actual cost?

1111. What was the actual budget or estimated cost for your organizations services?

1112. What is the average response time for answering a support call?

1113. If applicable; describe your standard schedule for new software version releases. Are new software version releases included in the standard maintenance plan?

1114. What are the minimum and optimal bandwidth

requirements for the proposed soluiton?

1115. What process manages the contracts?

1116. Who can list a Power purchase agreement project as organization experience, your organization or a previous employee of your organization?

1117. How is risk transferred?

4.6 Formal Acceptance: Power purchase agreement

1118. Have all comments been addressed?

1119. Do you perform formal acceptance or burn-in tests?

1120. Does it do what client said it would?

1121. Did the Power purchase agreement project achieve its MOV?

1122. What can you do better next time?

1123. Was the client satisfied with the Power purchase agreement project results?

1124. What are the requirements against which to test, Who will execute?

1125. Was the sponsor/customer satisfied?

1126. Do you buy-in installation services?

1127. What function(s) does it fill or meet?

1128. What features, practices, and processes proved to be strengths or weaknesses?

1129. Did the Power purchase agreement project manager and team act in a professional and ethical manner?

1130. Do you buy pre-configured systems or build your own configuration?

1131. Is formal acceptance of the Power purchase agreement project product documented and distributed?

1132. What is the Acceptance Management Process?

1133. Was the Power purchase agreement project goal achieved?

1134. General estimate of the costs and times to complete the Power purchase agreement project?

1135. Was the Power purchase agreement project work done on time, within budget, and according to specification?

1136. Does it do what Power purchase agreement project team said it would?

1137. Was business value realized?

5.0 Closing Process Group: Power purchase agreement

1138. What is the amount of funding and what Power purchase agreement project phases are funded?

1139. Was the user/client satisfied with the end product?

1140. What could have been improved?

1141. How will you know you did it?

1142. What is the Power purchase agreement project Management Process?

1143. If a risk event occurs, what will you do?

1144. Did you do things well?

1145. What areas does the group agree are the biggest success on the Power purchase agreement project?

1146. Did the Power purchase agreement project management methodology work?

1147. How well defined and documented were the Power purchase agreement project management processes you chose to use?

1148. Did the delivered product meet the specified requirements and goals of the Power purchase agreement project?

1149. Did you do what you said you were going to do?

1150. Mitigate. what will you do to minimize the impact should a risk event occur?

1151. Can the lesson learned be replicated?

1152. What areas were overlooked on this Power purchase agreement project?

5.1 Procurement Audit: Power purchase agreement

1153. Are rules in automatic disbursement programs adequate to prevent duplicate payment of invoices?

1154. Does your organization have an administrative timetable to assist the staff in implementing the budget calendar?

1155. Are all complaints of late or incorrect payment sent to a person independent of the already stated having cash disbursement responsibilities?

1156. Are the users needs clearly and invariably defined and has the expected outcome or mission been clearly identified and communicated in measurable terms?

1157. Could the bidders assess the economic risks the successful bidder would be responsible for, thus limiting the inclusion of extra charges for risk?

1158. Are there mechanisms for evaluating the departments suppliers performance in relation to prices, quality, delivery and innovation?

1159. Is it on a regular basis examined whether it is possible to enter into public private partnerships with private suppliers?

1160. Has your organization clearly defined the award criteria?

1161. Does the cash disbursement policy prohibit drawing checks to cash or bearer?

1162. Is there ineffective internal communication in the procurement function/unit?

1163. In open and restricted procedures, did the contracting authority make sure that there is no substantive change to the bid due to this clearing process?

1164. Are the right skills, experiences and competencies present in the acquisition workgroup and are the necessary outside specialists involved in part of the process?

1165. Is authorization required to make changes to the purchase order file?

1166. Is your organization aware and informed about international procurement standards and good practice?

1167. Was suitability of candidates accurately assessed?

1168. Are outsourcing and Public Private Partnerships considered as alternatives to in-house work?

1169. Are checks disbursed by someone other than the individual who authorized payment?

1170. Are risks managed to provide reasonable assurance regarding department procurement objectives?

1171. Was the award criteria that of the most economically advantageous tender?

1172. Are order quantities, deliveries and payment levels under the contract monitored by an appropriate official?

5.2 Contract Close-Out: Power purchase agreement

1173. Was the contract complete without requiring numerous changes and revisions?

1174. Was the contract sufficiently clear so as not to result in numerous disputes and misunderstandings?

1175. How does it work?

1176. Has each contract been audited to verify acceptance and delivery?

1177. Have all contract records been included in the Power purchase agreement project archives?

1178. Have all contracts been completed?

1179. Have all acceptance criteria been met prior to final payment to contractors?

1180. Have all contracts been closed?

1181. Change in attitude or behavior?

1182. How/when used ?

1183. Parties: Authorized?

1184. Was the contract type appropriate?

1185. Parties: who is involved?

1186. How is the contracting office notified of the automatic contract close-out?

1187. What is capture management?

1188. Are the signers the authorized officials?

1189. Change in circumstances?

1190. What happens to the recipient of services?

1191. Change in knowledge?

5.3 Project or Phase Close-Out: Power purchase agreement

1192. What stakeholder group needs, expectations, and interests are being met by the Power purchase agreement project?

1193. What can you do better next time, and what specific actions can you take to improve?

1194. What advantages do the an individual interview have over a group meeting, and vice-versa?

1195. What was expected from each stakeholder?

1196. What was learned?

1197. What are the informational communication needs for each stakeholder?

1198. What could be done to improve the process?

1199. Did the delivered product meet the specified requirements and goals of the Power purchase agreement project?

1200. How often did each stakeholder need an update?

1201. What information is each stakeholder group interested in?

1202. How much influence did the stakeholder have

over others?

1203. Who exerted influence that has positively affected or negatively impacted the Power purchase agreement project?

1204. What was the preferred delivery mechanism?

1205. Which changes might a stakeholder be required to make as a result of the Power purchase agreement project?

1206. Were risks identified and mitigated?

1207. Is the lesson significant, valid, and applicable?

1208. Was the schedule met?

5.4 Lessons Learned: Power purchase agreement

1209. Who had fiscal authority to manage the funding for the Power purchase agreement project, did that work?

1210. How effective was the architecture/system design process?

1211. How well were your expectations met regarding the extent of your involvement in the Power purchase agreement project (effort, time commitments, etc.)?

1212. How much flexibility is there in the funding (e.g., what authorities does the program manager have to change to the specifics of the funding within the overall funding ceiling)?

1213. Is your organization willing to expose problems or mistakes for the betterment of the collective whole, and can you do this in a way that does not intimidate employees or workers?

1214. Were the Power purchase agreement project objectives met (if not, briefly account for what wasnt met)?

1215. How effectively were issues resolved before escalation was necessary?

1216. How well does the product or service the Power purchase agreement project produced meet your needs?

1217. What Power purchase agreement project circumstances were not anticipated?

1218. Overall, how effective were the efforts to prepare you and your organization for the impact of the product/service of the Power purchase agreement project?

1219. Was the change control process properly implemented to manage changes to cost, scope, schedule, or quality?

1220. Who needs to learn lessons?

1221. Was sufficient time allocated to review Power purchase agreement project deliverables?

1222. Was the Power purchase agreement project manager sufficiently experienced, skilled, trained, supported?

1223. How was the quality of products/processes assured?

1224. For the next Power purchase agreement project, how could you improve on the way Power purchase agreement project was conducted?

1225. Is there any way in which you think your development process hampered this Power purchase agreement project?

1226. What were the main sources of frustration in the Power purchase agreement project?

1227. How efficient were Power purchase agreement project team meetings conducted?

1228. If you had to do this Power purchase agreement project again, what is the one thing that you would change (related to process, not to technical solutions)?

Index

Lightning Source UK Ltd.
Milton Keynes UK
UKHW021849050319
338544UK00008B/246/P

9 780655 513896